Tree Lines
21st Century American Poems

Tree Lines
21st Century American Poems

Jennifer Barber, Jessica Greenbaum, Fred Marchant
Editors

GRAYSON BOOKS
West Hartford, Connecticut
graysonbooks.com

Tree Lines: 21st Century American Poems
Copyright © 2022 Jennifer Barber, Jessica Greenbaum & Fred Marchant
ISBN: 978-1-7364168-8-4
Published by Grayson Books
West Hartford, Connecticut

Library of Congress Control Number: 2022932697
Book & Cover Design by Cindy Stewart
Cover Artwork by Neta Goren, "In Light of Woods," oil on canvas, 20x16 inches, 2010

for Jed, Peter, Stefi

Contents

INTRODUCTION: AMONG TREES *Jennifer Barber*   13

WHERE YOU ARE PLANTED

where you are planted   *Evie Shockley*   19

Choices   *Tess Gallagher*   20

Elegy beginning in the shade of Aunt Mary's
mulberry tree   *Camille T. Dungy*   21

The Way We Fled   *Eileen Cleary*   23

burial   *Ross Gay*   24

First Thought, Best Thought   *Andrea Cohen*   27

The Ayes Have It   *Tiana Clark*   28

Grief in Fenceposts   *Gary Whited*   30

74,000 Acres of Forest Burning   *Ellen Bass*   31

Inaugural Ball   *Jaswinder Bolina*   33

In the Forest of Splintered Trees   *Jean-Luc Fontaine*   35

Coat   *Kelle Groom*   36

Heave   *Yasmine Dalena*   37

from I Am a Miner. The Light Burns Blue   *Victoria Chang*   38

Balance, onslaught   *Khadijah Queen*   39

"Birds small enough…"   *Donald Revell*   40

Elegy on My Drive Home in the Rain
Laure-Anne Bosselaar   41

The Indiana Bats   *Cecily Parks*   43

Confessions of a nature lover   *Bob Hicok*   45

Rainforest   *Teresa Mei Chuc*   46

To the Old Maples   *Judy Katz*   47

Lord of Childhood   *D. Nurkse*   48

32 Views from the Hammock   *Lance Larsen*   49

Immortal Stories   *Diane Mehta*   50

In the Bronx   *Arthur Sze*   52

Hickory Nuts   *Barbara Thomas*   53

Conscious Sedation   *Kelly Cressio-Moeller*   54

Shore Cedars   *William Olsen*   55

from Eternity: *Landscape Painting*   *Tracy K. Smith*   57

Saguaros   *Javier Zamora*   58

ONE TREE

Green Figs   *Edward Hirsch*   61

What is Left   *Sy Hoahwah*   62

Taking Down the Tree   *Charles Coe*   63

In a Cemetery under a Solitary Walnut Tree
        That Crows   *Fady Joudah & Golan Haji*   64

So Different   *Kay Ryan*   65

The World's Oldest Cherry Tree Is Alive and Well
        But Barely Able to Walk   *Maya Janson*   66

Tree Ghost   *Yusef Komunyakaa*   67

Tree   *Jane Hirshfield*   68

Find the Hidden Tree   *Debora Lidov*   69

He Takes Me to See the Oldest Tree   *Lynne McMahon*   71

One Tree   *Philip Metres*   72

Coconuts   *Mihaela Moscaliuc*   73

Tree   *Vijay Seshadri*   74

Pine Tree Ode   *Sharon Olds*   75

Model of a Tree Growing in the Path of a Spiral   *Peter Streckfus*   76

The Storm-Struck Tree   *Jessica Greenbaum*   77

how to uproot a tree::   *Jennifer K. Sweeney*   78

Mistaking Silence for Consent   *Elizabeth J. Coleman*   79

The Tree   *Daniel Tobin*   80

Rudy's Tree   *Gail Mazur*   81

Pines   *James Richardson*   83

The Tree in the Midst   *John Shoptaw*   84

Ramón   *Frances Richey*   85

Peach Tree   *Connie Wanek*   86

The Oak Tree's Burden   *K.A. Moon*   87

My Father and the Figtree   *Naomi Shihab Nye*   88

Ant Tree   *Cheryl Savageau*   90

[From this bench I like to call my bench I sit]   *Diane Seuss*   91

Artifacts on a Hanging Tree, Goliad, Texas   *Anthony Cody*   92

What Isn't There   *Angela Narciso Torres*   93

Limen   *Natasha Trethewey*   94

Motion Harmony #2   *Jennifer Barber*   95

Copper Beech   *Geraldine Zetzel*   96

CALENDAR

The Cherries of Kenwood   *Ellen Kaufman*   99

White Petals, 3 A.M.   *Mary Jo Salter*   100

Dogwood Time   *Peter Marcus*   101

Gone   *Grace Schulman*   102

Autobiographia Literaria   *Elaine Sexton*   104

Cherry Blossoms   *Toi Derricotte*   106

Moved by the Beauty of the Trees   *Ishion Hutchinson*   108

In Lieu of Flowers   *Rebecca Okrent*   109

Forest and Trees   *Rachel Hadas*   110

Veil   *George Kalogeris*   111

Locust Trees in Late May   *Ted Kooser*   112

The Place des Vosges   *Richard Jones*   113

Mulberries in the Park   *Connie Wanek*   114

The Switch   *Maurice Manning*   115

The Marrow   *Rick Barot*   116

The Willow at Flint Pond   *Cheryl Savageau*   118

The Orchards   *Maxine Scates*   119

Shady Grove   *Don Share*   121

Floodplain   *Emily Tuszynska*   122

In the Second Half of Life   *Leslie Williams*   124

Cri de Coeur   *C. Dale Young*   125

The Problem of Describing Trees   *Robert Hass*   126

October   *David Ferry*   127

Watching Blackbirds Turn to Ghosts   *Rachel Eliza Griffiths*   128

Memento Mori: Apple Orchard   *Jennifer Franklin*   129

Monarchs, Viceroys, Swallowtails   *Robert Hedin*   130

Burnished Days   *John Koethe*   131

Fall   *Ed Ochester*   132

Leaf Litter   *Jennifer Markell*   133

Thinking of Frost   *Major Jackson*   134

October; November   *Alicia Suskin Ostriker*   135

Leaves   *Afaa Michael Weaver*   136

In November   *Alan Feldman*   137

The Grief of Trees   *Robin Becker*   139

Downdraft   *Carol Light*   141

Winter   *Esther Lin*   142

LISTENING, TELLING

The Trees   *Jericho Brown*   147

Corona (1)   *Sheila Black*   148

My City   *Khaled Mattawa*   149

Vertical   *Linda Pastan*   150

Mulberries   *Charles Coe*   151

Callimachus, Iamb 4, frag. 194   *Stephanie Burt*   153

It Begins with the Trees   *Ada Limón*   156

At the Cemetery   *Robert Cording*   158

[Parable]   *Leslie Harrison*   159

The Canopy   *Patricia Clark*   161

Alleluia   *Lynn Domina*   162

What I've Learned about Cottonwoods   *Gretchen Marquette*   163

Eulogy   *Brian Turner*   165

Ari in the Forest   *Howard Schwartz*   166

from *Blue Front*   *Martha Collins*   167

Trespass   *Jacquelyn Pope*   168

Lessons from a Tree   *Kim Stafford*   169

Cedar Theater   *Frances McCue*   170

New England Camping Ode   *Sharon Olds*   172

The Radiant's   *Arthur Sze*   174

Not Pigment, Not Truth   *Marsha Pomerantz*   175

Under the Linden   *Stephen Ackerman*   176

Humans Naming Trees   *Jessica Goodfellow*   177

Lobo   *Deborah Leipziger*   178

Cathedral   *Valencia Robin*   180

More desirable than gold [Psalm 19]   *Linda Zisquit*   181

from Pome: *Malus domestica*   *Erica Funkhouser*   182

Speaking Tree   *Joy Harjo*   184

Thinning the Spruces   *Jeffrey Harrison*   185

The Mostly Everything That Everyone Is   *Brenda Hillman*   187

Transmission   *Daniel Lawless*   189

The Discovery   *Lola Haskins*   190

Olive Harvest   *Fred Marchant*   191

The Etymology of Spruce   *Joyce Wilson*   192

For Chiara   *Rosanna Warren*   193

ABOUT THE POETS   195

PERMISSIONS   221

INDEX OF AUTHORS AND TITLES   235

Introduction: Among Trees

During the calamity of the past two years, I found myself thinking about trees. I felt a thirst for them and for reading poems about them. Something in the isolation we were living through had me seeing trees in a different way, not as static entities that make a passing scenic impression, but as embodiments of both the tangible and the infinitely unknowable.

I approached the poets and editors Jessica Greenbaum and Fred Marchant in the summer of 2020 with the idea of gathering new and recent poems that would shed light on these tangible and mysterious dimensions. We talked about the idea that trees, with their longer lifespans, are witnesses to history and connect us to geographic and cultural origins. We thought together about trees as generators of stories and as figures of contemplation and renewal. We also thought about them as markers of lifestyles. Who gets to spend time around trees, and who doesn't?

We were astonished by the range of tree poems in literary journals and in books, online, and straight from someone's desk. Sometimes a poet's work was known to one of us but not the others; sometimes we were all three encountering a new voice. Through these poems we traveled to cities, to playgrounds, to orchards and forests, to backyards and open fields. We immersed ourselves in poems which, through their proximity to one another, launched conversations about the complexities of identity and the occasional melting away of the self, about grieving, longing, and healing, and about praise, gratitude, and awe.

We've divided this volume into four parts. The first, "Where You Are Planted," which borrows its title from Evie Shockley's poem that opens the book, explores where we come from, and from whom, and how differences in class, race, gender, and regional backgrounds shape the landscape of our personal and collective histories.

The poems in the second part, "One Tree," zero in on a specific tree and the poet's relationship to it. While assembling this section, we thought about the passage from Martin Buber's *I and Thou* that begins with "I consider a tree," where he argues for the wholeness of the tree, the autonomy of its being, in opposition to the kind of knowledge that neatly categorizes but ends up distancing us from the tree's essential reality. Here you will encounter poems focused on a number of different species, each individual tree conjuring its own atmosphere: the world's oldest cherry tree, a plane tree in an urban park, an oak burdened by its role in a lynching almost a hundred years ago.

The third part, "Calendar," is attuned to weather and season. It starts with poems that describe the explosion of flower and leaf in spring and continues on with poems that usher in the days of summer and high summer, the arrival of fall's unmistakable transformations, and the stark silhouettes of winter. These poems understand that trees *are* calendars, bound up with our experience of passing time.

The fourth and final part is "Listening, Telling." By this we mean the poet's heightened awareness of what a tree or trees might be saying—to us, to other trees—and the lessons, broadly defined, that trees impart. Listening and telling are of critical importance if we are to understand our psychological, spiritual, and physical need for trees, and if we are, as a species, to adequately address the far-reaching environmental damage in progress. With this last in mind, the editors and publisher of this volume have made a commitment to donate a portion of the book's proceeds to the National Park Service Foundation.

We hope that as you read, you will fully enter the poems that are new to you and develop a deeper relationship with poems familiar to you from other contexts. Finally, we hope that by frequenting the worlds within worlds these poems bring into being, you will experience the presence of trees in a renewed light, and find your way among them, in words and in life.

—Jennifer Barber

Where You Are Planted

Evie Shockley

where you are planted

he's as high as a georgia pine, my father'd say, half laughing. southern trees
as measure, metaphor. highways lined with kudzu-covered southern trees.

fuchsia, lavender, white, light pink, purple: crape myrtle bouquets burst
open on sturdy branches of skin-smooth bark: my favorite southern trees.

one hundred degrees in the shade: we settle into still pools of humidity, moss-
dark, beneath live oaks. southern heat makes us grateful for southern trees.

the maples in our front yard flew in spring on helicopter wings. in fall, we
splashed in colored leaves, but never sought sap from these southern trees.

frankly, my dear, that's a magnolia, i tell her, fingering the deep green, nearly
plastic leaves, amazed how little a northern girl knows about southern trees.

i've never forgotten the charred bitter fruit of holiday's poplars, nor will i:
it's part of what makes me evie: i grew up in the shadow of southern trees.

Tess Gallagher

Choices

for Drago Štambuk

I go to the mountain side
of the house to cut saplings,
and clear a view to snow
on the mountain. But when I look up,
saw in hand, I see a nest clutched in
the uppermost branches.
I don't cut that one.
I don't cut the others either.
Suddenly, in every tree,
an unseen nest
where a mountain
would be.

Camille T. Dungy

Elegy beginning in the shade of Aunt Mary's mulberry tree

A week before the woman whose tree
  that golden dog was tied to died, I watched
my daughter trust its limbs. She sat still a long time
beyond reach of a buzzing that seemed to begin
  on the walk & grow louder near the front door.
  Thanksgiving is a word we use most often
in conjunction with feeling full nearly to excess.
  I mean what I felt witnessing that ascension—
  an ascension made by nearly every other child
who's grown up, even a little, around that house—
  seeing her trust her body doing something
  other bodies had already done. I am,
I hope you understand, not talking about my daughter.
  I need to remember how focused Aunt Mary was
on watching her body climbing so fast & so high.
There was something graceful in that ascension.
  This, too, is a way to speak about thanksgiving.
Her legs, her heart, her vision worked like necessary
magic. Then stopped. I can still taste the cool buttery skin
  of her forehead—though it's weeks ago now
I last kissed her. "Apple of my eye" I want to say
she called me, because she made me—some of you
  understand this—feel so deeply loved.
  But I can't put words in her mouth. The truth
is she craved peaches all summer. Fruit from the tree
  in her own yard wasn't anything anyone wanted
to eat. But the mulberry made for good climbing. Cast
cooling shade. The week after she died, it was some relief
  to stop pacing circles whose circumferences
measured our grief in time to see that retriever
  —leash wrapped at the place the trunk split.
She bounded & pranced in what we took to be wild

joy before we understood what truly moved her.
       Lord. Oh, Lord. Please understand how much—
       I think even now—the woman we loved loved
beautiful animals. What sense is there to make of this?
We watched that gorgeous creature run through the house
       out to the other yard. She'd been released
       from the lead that kept her tied to a suffering
that came down on her body as a mad hornet swarm.
No sense in this either, but as we watched her pass
       we could have sworn she was still dancing.

Eileen Cleary

The Way We Fled

No branch
silhouettes the snow.

Tree limbs cut down by some bastard or buzz saw,
chipped remains scattered

afield around the stump
as if they'd tried to escape

the carnage, the way we fled
from my father after school.

Our legs gave out.
He'd gather our grains in a burlap sack,

sprinkle us around the corners of the house,
soak his roots in whiskey.

If you ever find you are defenseless

it's best to compliment the buzz saw,
caress its teeth—

pour it a glass of Jack Daniels. Let it snarl.
Wait for the roars to become wheezes.

Then, walk from the field. Unhurried.

Ross Gay

burial

You're right, you're right,
the fertilizer's good—
it wasn't a gang of dullards
came up with chucking
a fish in the planting hole
or some midwife got lucky
with the placenta—
oh, I'll plant a tree here!—
and a sudden flush of quince
and jam enough for months—yes,
the magic dust our bodies become
casts spells on the roots
about which someone else
could tell you the chemical processes,
but it's just magic to me,
which is why a couple of springs ago
when first putting in my two bare root plum trees
out back I took the jar which has become
my father's house,
and lonely for him and hoping to coax him back
for my mother as much as me,
poured some of him in the planting holes
and he dove in glad for the robust air,
saddling a slight gust
into my nose and mouth,
chuckling as I coughed,
but mostly he disappeared
into the minor yawns in the earth
into which I placed the trees,
splaying wide their roots,
casting the gray dust of my old man
evenly throughout the hole,
replacing then the clods

of dense Indiana soil until the roots
and my father were buried,
watering it in all with one hand
while holding the tree
with the other straight as the flag
to the nation of simple joy
of which my father is now a naturalized citizen,
waving the flag
from his subterranean lair,
the roots curled around him
like shawls or jungle gyms, like
hookahs or the arms of ancestors,
before breast-stroking into the xylem,
riding the elevator up
through the cambium and into the leaves where,
when you put your ear close enough,
you can hear him whisper
good morning, where, if you close your eyes
and push your face you can feel
his stubbly jowls and good lord
this year he was giddy at the first
real fruit set and nestled into the 30 or 40 plums
in the two trees, peering out from the sweet meat
with his hands pressed against the purple skin
like cathedral glass,
and imagine his joy as the sun
wizarded forth those abundant sugars
and I plodded barefoot
and prayerful at the first ripe plum's swell and blush,
almost weepy conjuring
some surely ponderous verse
to convey this bottomless grace,
you know, *oh father oh father* kind of stuff,
hundreds of hot air balloons
filling the sky in my chest, replacing his intubated body
listing like a boat keel side up, replacing
the steady stream of water from the one eye

which his brother wiped before removing the tube,
keeping his hand on the forehead
until the last wind in his body wandered off,
while my brother wailed like an animal,
and my mother said, weeping,
it's ok, it's ok, you can go honey,
at all of which my father
guffawed by kicking from the first bite
buckets of juice down my chin,
staining one of my two button-down shirts,
the salmon-colored silk one, hollering
there's more of that!
almost dancing now in the plum,
in the tree, the way he did as a person,
bent over and biting his lip
and chucking the one hip out
then the other with his elbows cocked
and fists loosely made
and eyes closed and mouth made trumpet
when he knew he could make you happy
just by being a little silly
and sweet.

Andrea Cohen

First Thought, Best Thought

I'm three or four,
hidden in the branches

of the cherry tree.
I don't ask: how

did I get here?
I don't fear falling.

The job of the blossoms
is to bloom, to be

beautifully unschooled in ruin.

Tiana Clark

The Ayes Have It

When I think of Trayvon Martin, I think of Emmett Till,
    when I think of Emmett Till, I think of young, black men
        in the South,

then I think of young, white men in the South.
    I think of my husband, who is white, born and raised in
        Franklin, TN.

I think of how when he tries to hold my hand,
    sometimes I pull away and not because I don't love him,

but because I'm alert, I think of other people,
    other people who are born in the South,

that remember the Old South, and in fact long for it.
    I think about the nooses that hung on our back porch

when I was little: one for me and one for my mom,
    I think about how people say

It's not about race, don't make it about race,
    I wish black people would stop talking about race!

When all I've ever known is being defined by my race.
    What are you? Where are you from?

I say *California*, but that's not what they are looking for—
    they are asking about my parents.

What they want to know is that my mother is black
    and my dad is white. *I'm mixed.*

So when I think about a post-racial America, I don't—
    because the trees in the South have strange fruit histories,

the roots are deep red, tangled and gnarled, so again—
    when I think of Trayvon, I think of hoodies, then I think

of stereotypes, I think of skittles and high fructose corn syrup,
    tasting the rainbow, and then I think of gay marriage,

then just marriage in general and then I'm back to my husband,
    and see he's trying to hold my hand again, but the truth is
        I'm scared.

Because I have to love him differently in the South,
    just like young, black men have to exist differently in the South,

they can't just wink at any woman, Mr. Till,
    just walk through any neighborhood, Mr. Martin,

just wear any hoodie, buy any iced tea. Someone is watching,
    always watching us, so when I think about justice,

I think about eyeballs, the first impression,
    the action that follows, George Zimmerman stepping

out of his car. I think what would have happened
    if he'd just given him a ride home?

Gary Whited

Grief in Fenceposts

I felt its reach riding horseback
in summer pastures, passing by
the proud posts always standing

at the spot where they were set,
holding the barbed wire under
the wounding staples.

Each post, once a tree that stood
along some creek, knows every sunrise
to sunset, each moon's wax and wane,

every season, every storm, the cow,
the deer, the meadowlark and hawk,
rattlesnake, magpie, badger and horse.

The grief in fenceposts, I felt it
pass into my own upright body,
learned trust at the side of each post,

and what I desire now, to stand, naked,
seeing everything from where I am,
faithful to the place.

Ellen Bass

74,000 Acres of Forest Burning

The kids go out for coffee. They arrived at 3 AM and we only have decaf.

They've left chimneys in the rubble. Contorted washers and driers.

The blistered street sign. The flaming heart of the redwood.

Even here, the air hangs umber-colored, smoke-thickened.

Ash falls, flaking the bench, the path. It gathers in the veins of leaves, in the spiders' webs.

Sally carries photos and notebooks from the car and the lace wedding dress she still hasn't worn.

Max brings a big bowl of heirloom tomatoes and his knives.

Janet bakes an apple galette and cries.

Here we tunnel into the day. Here we shovel the hours.

I walk the neighborhood, crushing a thin crust.

A man sleeps in his car, seat tilted back.

A woman stands at the open door of her van. Inside chickens flutter in cages. She gives them water.

Back home, kibbles in the dog's bowl.

The sun is neon orange on our kitchen wall.

I pack a tinted photo of my mother, Janet's silver bracelets, the ceramica we schlepped the length of Italy.

Sally vacuums.

Now she thinks she feels the baby move.

We strain toward the next briefing. The fire's moving on the ridge. It's
.8 miles from their house.

I cut parsley from the garden, wash off the greasy film.

Bees keep on nuzzling into the blossoms.

An ant carries a broken ant across the patio.

A fire truck. Four men in profile through the windows. They look
straight ahead, jaws set.

The dahlias nod their big flame-heads in the breeze that's picking up.

Breeze is what we don't want. The maple leaves rustle.

Jaswinder Bolina

Inaugural Ball

Elsewhere,
the carpenter

must rip and strip
the pine into lumber,

must plane and miter
his planks and assemble

the tiny caskets,
the toddler-shaped

ones, must stack them
into ranks and columns

against walls
of his workshop

to the prim cadence
of an overnight World

Service anchor
on the shortwave,

must print his invoice
and deliver it

to whoever cuts
the checks, whosoever

settles the accounts
payable as the populist

spins and grips and dips
his flinching bride.

Jean-Luc Fontaine

In the Forest of Splintered Trees

The winter I saw a tree explode, my father took me hunting in the fir-pregnant forest behind our house—anxiety throbbing in my forehead, like an eel trapped under tarp, as my father made me struggle through the snow with his rifle. Past the clearing I heard the crack of bark and cowered into snow as bits of wood arrowed all around, like hornets disturbed from their slumber—a tree splintered down the middle, a large gap between the boughs. Don't overreact, my father told me as he pulled me up by the scrunch of my jacket. It's just frozen sap expanding. I could hear the trees erupting all throughout that long slog through the bone-white snow. That whole winter I heard them: the ruptures forming, the sap pulsing from the wood. Even now, I catch the buckle of bark, like when gridlocked in traffic, slamming the stumps of my fists against the steering wheel, or when cut in line at the post office—my toes digging into the soles of my shoes, like roots desperate for water.

Kelle Groom

Coat

A coat hung in a pine tree outside my bedroom window
like a seamless tan nightgown

displayed in the 1977 Kansas City exhibition
of North American Indian Art—the Algonquin coat or Cree

from the early nineteenth century, pre-reservation,
mooseskin coat with caribou, red and gray pain washed

away, the porcupine quills a woman chewed and softened
in her mouth, sewed on the shoulders, come loose.

I walked into the grass to get a closer look,
and a man in a blue truck stopped on the quiet dirt,

asked if I had seen a moose.
He'd found tracks up in the field

where the hunters park their campers.
No, but here is his thin coat, moving and alive,

waving as if on a clothesline,
waving like so many leaves.

Yasmine Dalena

Heave

Settled in the swings, his girls
push their toes against the grass,
then pitch their heels into the air.

With each pass, the A-frames tilt
before the loosened posts
hammer back into the ground.

His brothers come to build the tree-house
in his place. He left a skeleton
of redwood boards and braces.

Against the sawing and the nailing,
his girls still batter at the clouds
and sling their bodies to the sky.

Victoria Chang

from I Am a Miner. The Light Burns Blue

An old man   pushes up   a clavicle of   a lime tree

only the   ashes know why   they   fall from his

cigarette like   asterisks   he doesn't look up   our bodies

and   strollers overlap   fresh cement steams   against

stucco homes and   new sod   babies' faces   reflect on

storefronts   our skin   like   cactuses   we are

latched to   this   landscape   where trees   need

wooden sticks to   stand   straight   where workers trim

thistles   on the trail   each day working   their way

west   and   back   where fields are   aerated into

Chinese checker boards   plugs of   brown dirt strewn

like   confetti like something to   celebrate   where

we try   to shed   ruin   at daylight   but   by   nightfall

our   hands   are always wilderness

Khadijah Queen

Balance, onslaught

after Clare Rojas

(I have a diamond house
with men. I have pierced
men and diamond shoes.
I have shoed horses and
a tilted head. I have a tilted
cart and a flowered scarf.
I have a gray dress and a
hell of a guitar. I play the
guitar and the jukebox jack-
in-the-box gutted brown
bear and canoe landscape. I
play the grayest song and a
cat's yarn game.) I sit in the
forest with a cat and a knife.
(I see the quilted mountains
and long knitted birds. I see
the man limping across the
path of chevrons between
the trees. I sit between trees,
hanging hair and red mouth.
I mouth and sit. The buck
stands by the river. I am in
my paper mask, my wood.)

Donald Revell

"Birds small enough…"

Birds small enough to nest in our young cypress
Are physicians to us

They burst from the tree exactly
Where the mind ends and the eye sees

Another world the equal of this one
Though only a small boy naked in the sun

Glad day glad day I was born
Sparrow hatted old New York

And the physician who brought me
Drowned under sail next day in a calm sea

There are birds small enough to live forever
Where the mind ends and where

My love and I once planted a cypress
Which is God to us

Laure-Anne Bosselaar

Elegy on My Drive Home in the Rain
for Larry Levis

When it rains on Las Positas Road,
   the trunk of a eucalyptus there turns
  blue—with a few blood-red streaks—but mostly
    blue: a bright
      hard cobalt,

   & it just stands there, bleeding that blue,
among the other eucalyptus in their safe
     camouflage of beige & brown—

& I remember something Larry wrote about Caravaggio,
  how he painted his own face
      in the decapitated head of Goliath,

  & how Larry wanted *to go up to it & close both eyelids*
   because they were *still half-open & it seemed a little obscene*
            to leave them like that.

        ☞

   I planted a willow in a garden in Belgium when Larry died.
It grew by blue-painted shutters. I wanted that tree
   to keep weeping there after I left for America again—

America who had lost Larry too—& I thought about that,
      & about his two trees, lost somewhere
   in Utah—the *acer negundo* he wrote,
& the other one whose name he could never remember.

   So that now when I drive home I think of those trees:
the *acer negundo*, the other one, & my willow.

Brother limitation races beside me like a shadow too, Larry,
      so that now, when it rains,

I take another way home, or look
                                        away
from the Las Positas eucalyptus
standing there soaked & so bleeding so blue.
                    It seems *a little obscene to leave it like that.*

Cecily Parks

The Indiana Bats

They're like little brown handkerchiefs waving goodbye
in the sky. Goodbye oaks, dogwoods, ashes and elms.
Goodbye, caves. Goodbye, mines and the coal
that lit up the night. Goodbye, night that the bats fly by.

The bats fly by twilight, or bat-light, and their bat-flight is full
of waltz and veer and feeding in midair. Goodbye,
arcane glide over the woodlot. Goodbye, tiny pink tongue
that drinks on the wing from the pond with the apricot glow.

The apricot glow fills the carriage window of the overnight train
rushing two fields away and then (Goodbye!) it's too late
to ask who's inside or what they're saying. The bats
hear sumac, nettle, and wild grape when a woman hears nothing.

A woman hears that elves wear bat-fur coats, or witches
cook with wool of bat, and goodbye, Dunsinane. Goodbye,
the old wives say, believing that when a bat flies into a woman's hair,
she hears voices that remain indefinite, and goes insane.

Voices that remain indefinite reverberate through the cloister
of hickories and bounce off the goldenrod and poison ivy. They
compose the stream, the fall-flowering anemones, and the
    mosquito's wing,
indexing the distance between the hawthorn and extinction.

Because the tincture of night is darkened by their goodbyes:
"My umbrella was cut in half," says one. "Goodbye, havens
and hibernacula," says another. "I never knew a belfry," says one.
"I spent my whole life shouting hello," says another.

Say another goodbye to the bat hanging in the shower
before an adult with a badminton racquet flushes it down the toilet.

Say one goodbye to the derelict gabled mansion where signs
warned people never to touch the bats sleeping on the ceiling.

Sleep with me, the bats sing each winter before hibernation.
Sleep with me, sings the baby bat to its mother in the roost
in the bark of the decaying maple tree. Sleep with me, the maple sings,
having said goodbye to making leaves and green twisting keys.

Bob Hicok

Confessions of a nature lover

Back then I was going steady
with fog, who could dance
like no one's business, I threw her over
for a leaf that one day fluttered
first her shadow then her whole life
into my hand, that's a lot
of responsibility and a lot
of relatives, this leaf
and that leaf and all the other leaves
hung around, I told her
I needed space, which was true,
without it I'd only be a soul,
and no one's sure that wisp
is real, that's why we say
of real estate, location, location,
location, and of speech,
locution, locution, locution,
and of love, yes, yes, yes,
and I am on my knees, will you have me,
world?

Teresa Mei Chuc

Rainforest

I close my eyes so that I can see it.
What we freely eliminate. Who is

not guilty of it? We reek of paper.
Everywhere we go is paper. Our

hands are stained with paper.
Walls. What echoes from our walls.

The sweet whisper of rainforest—
even the name makes the sound of

rushing water or perhaps it's a ghost
that haunts us. They say the dead

that did not die a peaceful death are
doomed forever to wander the earth.

But perhaps this earth is for them
already a cemetery—stacks and

stacks of flesh on a desk. Which
one belongs to which tree?

Already, we've traded oxygen for
so much.

Judy Katz

To the Old Maples

We caught the end
of your lives and didn't know it,
you who sold us on this house.
We drove up and you were talking
among yourselves, wide-trunked,
stately, not the least bit stuffy.
Gorgeous. Gossiping.
In summer you shaded us, whispered
to each other as we rocked in the hammock,
no one keeping track.
It must be terrible to see each other go
in a few short winters—
even harder than it's been for us
to lose you. I remember the first
ground-out stump in the backyard.
It had snowed early that year
and Mike Root (his real name)
had taken you down. I came outside
and saw a gash in the earth, ground up
pulp, mercurochrome red, bleeding
through the snow.
Then one after the next, huge limbs
sheared off by wind,
crowns cracked and splintering, heavy
branches hanging by the very wires
used to secure you.

D. Nurkse

Lord of Childhood

We are all enchanted. But we have to pay for it.

You know that part of town where the miners once lived? Sooty frame houses, porches whose floorboards spring up? Rusty screen doors that close with a thrum, then a series of clicks, then a squeak?

There you find the padlocked sweatshops. The names of things they once made have been worn blank by the north wind. Imagine you can read: doorknob. Comb. Shoehorn. Or your fingertips can trace the groove the letters etched.

The factory that produced thimbles is bricked in. The threadworks has no roof.

All the streets are named for trees: Pine, Cedar, Elm, Maple. There are only sagging chainlink fences. At the corner of Birch and Willow a Corvette is double-parked. A boy squats by the trunk. He has the dust. You buy it with something from your parents' house. The ormolu lamp. The clock with a pendulum. The portrait with its massive gilt frame. How I wanted to keep the face. Just take the gold leaf and smelt it. But no. The face comes too.

Now I am enchanted, like a raven in a story, a deer, a tiger, a toad. Eras pass like a hand sweeping over a clock dial: tweets, updates, cities lost, besieged, bombarded.

Some nights I see the Lord, stacking bills in his golden window. Should I ring the bell and beg: give me back my father's face?

Lance Larsen

32 Views from the Hammock

1. Solstice, and still the maples are flaunting their green tresses.
2. The smoky gossip of burning trash.
3. A mug of yesterday's tepid jasmine tea.
4. What passes as shade: the drifting jibber-jabber of clouds.
5. A hammock and a man are one.
6. A hammock and a man and his wife's shoulders are one.
7. Not her actual shoulders, which are in Cincinnati this week.
8. But his freckled memory of them.
9. Next door, a trampoline launches a boy into the blue.
10. Not on my watch, says gravity.
11. Visit again real soon, says the air.
12. Closer to earth, a fountain pleasures itself and gathers bees.
13. A mantis interviews a cricket, one bite at a time.
14. Sheets snapping in lavender praise.
15. The crime is not Bartok or the piano or little girl hands.
16. Blame the window, that busybody open window.
17. Poor ant: trundling home a moth as big as a sail boat.
18. Like much in life, wings are metaphor.
19. So many leaves, so many shivery prayers.
20. Free sky miles, says the sky—use them.
21. Distant thunder, like God re-shelving books.
22. Will this pile of gravel ever become a path?
23. Do some angles of repose double as tipping points?
24. Whose tragedy does that dying siren usher in?
25. You call this a nap?
26. Questions like these—they wear me out.
27. Fit *man, hammock,* and *longing* into one sentence—never.
28. Why not? His beloved's shoulders won't hold still.
29. Do guardian angels choose whom they haunt?
30. Rain, some say, is an aphrodisiac.
31. Teach me, teach me tonight.
32. Inside, the tea pot whistles, as if gathering our lost ones home.

Diane Mehta

Immortal Stories

In this city of crows and rose-ringed parakeets,
elephants and camels labor down the beach,
marionettes tell stories in knotted banyan trees.
Old monkeys with young men, men-monkeys in old stories
more pure than whatever we believe.
For a half-century I wandered the Hanging Gardens
where one farmer and topiary animals are stuck in their cosmology.
Monsoons blow by, the dead disintegrate and find new lives.
Still they hold their shapes.
The topiary farmer will never plow his field.
He treadwheels the same triangular plot of grass,
tilling the same immortal land
under cloudless skies or fat rains.
He has witnessed new irrigation and exports of tea,
arrivals of King George and Queen Mary
for which the water's edge jetty
blossomed into the basalt arch that is,
for ordinary souls, the Gateway of India.
The farmer has listened quietly as millworkers
lurched from red-light rooms to wives
spreading love. He has seen famine and plenty,
the arrival of antibiotics, the purge of syphilis.
He has agitated for self-rule in his photosynthesis heart,
he has marched with his plow
in demonstrations from the start.
He has seen the blood-burst of Partition.
He is destined to be cut and trimmed
again. So much for love, he thinks, it is not here
any more than I am.
He is doing the work of life, he will never reach Nirvana
though he will pray forever.
A peacock calls the operatic light
in a field behind the two-acre forest our gardener built

near the shanties that rose under the palm trees and skyscrapers
that Nehru built. I am sailing to my old Bombay
of my oldest dreams, into my aunt's cosmos so antique
it resembles neither the beginning nor the end of time,
only the building blocks of matter
where principles of motion and rest are divine,
which brings us to the topiary man and his plow
pressing infinitely on.
There is a light show in the fountain in the evenings.
The farmer feels all four seasons on his hedge-skin
as if teasing him to join the human feelings.
The field needs tending, he says, eyes lowered,
and leans into his plow.
I retreat as sundown lifts over the hill.
Oh what promise this passport permits.
I am no longer lovely.
People chatter on in more dialects than I remember.
I am visiting my old home on the fifth floor
with its salt-sea view and terrace of my parakeets.
Up the street the topiary man is still plowing and plowing his field.

Arthur Sze

In the Bronx

Crossing a street, you hear the cry of a strawberry finch,
               and, reaching the curb,

catch the smell of a young pig that, minutes ago,
               hurtled across the trail;

inhaling a chocolate scent, you approach a small orchid;
               nearby, two streaked

pitcher plants have opened lids but opened laterally;
               a fern rises out

of the crotch of an ʻōhiʻa tree, and droplets have collected
               on a mule's foot fern;

up on the ridge, sliding mist veils the palms and eucalyptus;
               nearby, a trumpet tree

dangles orange-scented blooms; you stare at the crack
               in a blue marble tree,

at a maze of buttressed roots, just as a man holding
               a placard, waving people

toward a new doughnut shop, turns and, thud, a wild avocado
               has dropped to the ground.

Barbara Thomas

Hickory Nuts

Be careful, Mom says, zipping up our jackets,
Don't talk to strangers.
Grabbing buckets, we trot downhill,
cross the bridge where whitewater churns over the dam,
the roar of the river in our ears as we walk up Mooth's Hill.

We pluck hickory nuts snug in thick brown husks,
peel some, crush inner shells with a hefty stone
for tender morsels inside,
savor the bits of tastiness.
The air smells of dusty leaves and sunshine.

When our pails are almost full, a black pick-up truck approaches,
the driver slows down watching us.
We remember what our mother said and turn our backs.
Don't talk to strangers, it might be the hunter.
The hunter, the hunter, we sing.

Kelly Cressio-Moeller

Conscious Sedation

Slipping under, I remember me—
a girl neglectful of the sky,

wearing red Mary Janes
and a full set of teeth. Now I walk

through shadows of tall trees, their clinquant
boughs gold and silver crowned.

My breath warm on the pane of a glasswing
butterfly as I lean in to hear the heartbeat

of a wych elm, frisk the bark for a pig's tooth
to replace the tender rogue in my jaw—

another gone before it is taken,
another taken before I am gone.

William Olsen

Shore Cedars

Three weeks trying to find an analogy for…
not the cedars;
                       but their singular branches
while earth waits us out.

Each branch is a cedar tree
                           rooted in cedar sap,
slow, indescribable sap,
slow interior coursework.

Teaches Sound spits up and smooths over.
                                  Gone with saying,
gone without saying, it smooths,
the wind off the smooth
                  so smooth a talker

it doesn't make any waves.
The water waking to blue,
                  our willed change,
were we ever even here?

Posthumous existence consumes them.
Salt kill, prune our limbs,
                  trim our corkscrew wicks,
spray and scab us with lichen.

There was calm behind the wind
and calm before wind, only
across a calm consent did wind
                    blow away deadfall,

trouble even the green shoreward branches,
small-hearted Carolina wrens:

unheard pulses. Unclenched,
                                clenched, unclenching.

Tracy K. Smith

from Eternity: *Landscape Painting*

It is as if I can almost still remember.
As if I once perhaps belonged here.

The mountains a deep heavy green, and
The rocky steep drop to the waters below.

The peaked roofs, the white-plastered
Brick. A clothesline in a neighbor's yard

Made of sticks. The stone path skimming
The ridge. A ladder asleep against a house.

What is the soul allowed to keep? Every
Birth, every small gift, every ache? I know

I have knelt just here, torn apart by loss. Lazed
On this grass, counting joys like trees: cypress,

Blue fir, dogwood, cherry. Ageless, constant,
Growing down into earth and up into history.

Javier Zamora

Saguaros

It was dusk for kilometers and bats in the lavender sky,
       like spiders when a fly is caught, began to appear.

And there, not the promised land, but barbwire and barbwire
       with nothing growing under it. I tried to fly that dusk

after a bat said *la sangre del saguaro nos seduce.* Sometimes
       I wake and my throat is dry, so I drive to the botanical gardens

to search for red fruit clutched to saguaros, the ones at dusk
       I threw rocks at for the sake of slashing hunger.

But I never find them here. These bats say *speak English only.*
       Sometimes in my car, that viscous red syrup

clings to my throat, and it's a tender seed toward my survival:
       I also scraped needles first, then carved those tall torsos

for water, then spotlights drove me and thirty others dashing
       into palos verdes, green-striped trucks surrounded us,

our empty bottles rattled and our breath spoke with rust.
       When the trucks left, a cold cell swallowed us.

One Tree

Edward Hirsch

Green Figs

I want to live like that little fig tree
    that sprouted up at the beach last spring
        and spread its leaves over the sandy rock.

All summer its stubborn green fruit
    (tiny flowers covered with a soft skin)
        ripened and grew in the bright salt spray.

The Tree of the Knowledge of Good
    and Evil was a fig tree, or so it is said,
        but this wild figure was a wanton stray.

I need to live like that crooked tree—
    solitary, bittersweet, and utterly free—
        that knelt down in the hardest winds

but could not be blasted away.
    It kept its eye on the far horizon
        and brought honey out of the rock.

Sy Hoahwah

What is Left

What is left

of my family's 160 acres:
a lone pecan tree
on the fringe of Cache Creek

A squirrel runs up and down
the trunk

carrying insults

between my dead grandfather
and the birds that live

in the top branches.

I carve my name
on the moon's teeth.

Charles Coe

Taking Down the Tree

A few days after my father's funeral I saw a dead tree cut down,
an ancient leafless oak, surrounded by men in hard hats and goggles,
gathered like wolves at a bear's carcass. Drivers passed slowly,
hypnotized by the stream of wood flowing from the chipper.

An old man and his dog stopped to watch; the man leaned against
a fence, arms folded, face unreadable; the dog sniffed as the ghosts
of a billion leaves, a silent funeral train, floated by in the cool
        morning air.

Fady Joudah & Golan Haji

In a Cemetery under a Solitary
Walnut Tree That Crows

had planted and whose seeds are hollow
I found a needle and with it

I dug a well dug
and dug until I struck ink

The needle wove fabric for bodies it had injected with song
I painted the well's walls with quicklime and couldn't climb out

There was sun there was moonlight that came into my sleep
I stored leaves and bark but rain washed away my words

A lantern came down on a rope that a girl held
I sent up the part of me that was light

Kay Ryan

So Different

A tree is lightly connected
to its blossoms.
For a tree it is
a pleasant sensation
to be stripped
of what's white and winsome.
If a big wind comes,
any nascent interest in fruit
scatters. This is so different
from humans, for whom
what is un-set matters
so oddly—as though
only what is lost held possibility.

Maya Janson

The World's Oldest Cherry Tree Is Alive and Well But Barely Able to Walk

Word is, the villagers have fashioned special sticks to prop it up,
to keep its 1000-year-old hat from falling to the ground.

Everyone wants to picnic beneath its waterfall
and laugh about the petals that fall into their drinks.

There's a Japanese word for that, for the progressive and manifest
degrees of flowering and drunkenness beneath the boughs.

Another word for, roughly translated, *you-must-put-your-nose-right-into-the-blossom-to-practice-and-perfect-your-bee.*

When I visited I rode my bike past narrow canals and thought—
just like Holland, where I've never been.

Pedaled right through the middle of a discourse
two young scholars were having about flexibility as they leaned

against the smallest tree in the orchard. Underfoot,
the spring grass was an animal whose fur must never be cut.

This by Emperor's decree. It rubbed itself against
the ankles of the revelers, the loud, red ones and the quiet ones

who stood there looking straight into the swirling cascade
and saw up close how the world was made.

Yusef Komunyakaa

Tree Ghost

There's a rush, a rustle
among branches of a conifer,
& then mutable silence rushes in
like after a fight or making love.
The wings settle. The third eye
blindfolded. Hunger always speaks
the same language. Branches shudder
overhead & the snowy owl's wingspan
seems to cool off the August night
with a breathing in & breathing out.
I close my eyes & can still see
the three untouched mice dead
along the afternoon footpath.
The screeching nest is ravenous.
The mother's claws grab a limb.
Now, what I know makes me look down
at the ground. I can almost feel
how the owl's beauty scared the mice
to death, how the shadow of her wings
was a god passing over the grass.

Jane Hirshfield

Tree

It is foolish
to let a young redwood
grow next to a house.

Even in this
one lifetime,
you will have to choose.

That great calm being,
this clutter of soup pots and books—

Already the first branch-tips brush at the window.
Softly, calmly, immensity taps at your life.

Debora Lidov

Find the Hidden Tree

When you try to think about the tree
in the small front yard,
all you see are the blue-painted steps and porch;
and the more you know about the tree,
the less you can see it was a maple,
which makes metaphorical sense
because your maple was the biggest on the block
but you coveted willows on other blocks,
their long tangled tresses and their weeping.
If it's 1979, all you'll see
is the woman in distress on the chipped blue stairs—
leaf in hand, semi-starred and turgid,
the two-bladed seed pods
helicoptering down.
Sirens sounding, whirling lights.
But when you try to describe the man
who flashed you last July
in Brooklyn's Mt. Prospect park,
July of the already famous 2020,
summer between the first wave and second wave,
all you see is the tree.
You were sunning yourself in the grass,
and he was standing off, by the oak.
At first, he acted afraid.
You took him for itchy or addicted;
he was squirrely, glancing, tugging at his shirt in the heat,
and so to give him his space
to shoot up or freak out, you thought,
and assurance you wouldn't report him,
you lay back and looked up,
angled your middle-aged progressives just so
at the jagged predictable edges of
the almost oval leaves,

the edges so far away
but your glasses so capable of finding.
And when you search yourself for regret
you settle on your year out West.
You were age 18 and living in San Francisco
and traveled only once to see the redwoods.
You wanted to belong to the redwoods.
You wanted to want the redwoods,
but all you felt was awe.
Nobody knows you worship a forest
you couldn't stand to inhabit.
And nobody knows that you journey
back to Mt. Prospect today
and put your arms today around the trunk
where your young flasher recently leaned
and steadied his squirrely nerves
before he lowered his pants and stroked himself for you,
before you sat up and saw
and fled from him, defending him. He's harmless,
you muttered. They're always harmless,
your oak and you agree. Nobody sees you,
weeping, returning, hugging its trunk.
An actual hugger you are—
your face against the bark, your eyes firmly closed:
Everyone is gone.
Everyone is well.

Lynne McMahon

He Takes Me to See the Oldest Tree

          in Missouri, a burr oak, the oxidized plaque
faintly states, which so dominates the landscape
          he calls it Wordsworth
(there's even a companion oak across the road,
also gigantic, and nearly equal in girth,
          Coleridgian in its effort to be
               the other tree or have, at least,

          the other tree acknowledge it). The field
is lipped in tansy, planted in soy, only eight miles
          on the old railroad bed,
and we're on bikes, a nothing hike in Wordsworth's
day, but I'm out of breath by the time we stop,
          and whatever oblation I've brought runs down
               my throat instead.

          He's led me here for vastness's sake
and elegy: "but there's a Tree, of many, one
          a single Field which I
have looked upon…" But what's gone from me
is not yet here, only hinted at today—my father's failing
          memory, my mother's anxious heart,
               and the part of the poem

          I most want to keep
is the meanest flower, which he takes for me
          and places in a Krinos jar
to carry home "in the holiness of the heart's
affection," as Keats once said. Not for the dead,
          but for our own bodies
               in our marriage bed.

Philip Metres

One Tree

They wanted to tear down the tulip tree, our neighbors, last year. It throws a shadow over their vegetable patch, the only tree in our backyard. We said no. Now they've hired someone to chainsaw an arm—the crux on our side of the fence—and my wife, in tousled hair and morning sweats, marches to stop the carnage, mid-limb. It reminds her of her childhood home, a shady place to hide. She recites her litany of no, returns. Minutes later, the neighbors emerge. The worker points to our unblinded window. I want to say, it's not me, slide out of view behind a wall of cupboards, ominous breakfast table, steam of tea, our two young daughters now alone. I want no trouble. Must I fight for my wife's desire for yellow blooms when my neighbors' tomatoes will stunt and blight in shade? Always the same story: two people, one tree, not enough land or light or love. Like the baby brought to Solomon, someone must give. Dear neighbor, it's not me. Bloom-shadowed, light-deprived, they lower the chainsaw again.

Mihaela Moscaliuc

Coconuts

Las Terrenas, Dominican Republic

He says he holds the record
as the fastest climber,
eighteen seconds, eighty feet up,
tender-footed on the trunk,
and before I get to wonder
he's straddling its shoulders,
machete between lips, small knife
whoknowswhere, and off fly
droopy fronds till the top
shakes and sways like a girl
testing newfound weightlessness
in the salon mirror—
then the blade visible
in the fall that precedes
the sliding body
preceded
          by the cluster of heads
I've purchased in advance,
robust with heavenly water,
lethal in descent.

Vijay Seshadri

Tree
for Richard Wilbur

Three streets south of where I sit
is a city park with a plane tree in it.

From any place you choose to enter,
the tree forms the park's pole and perfect center.

Its slight, heliotropic, side-
wise bias, its height, and its wide,

rustling canopy all testify that it has won
its long negotiations with the sun,

and now simply distributes the breeze,
and keeps guard over these

ruminant people who stand before
the local memorial to the war

or sit on benches ordering the mess
and stilling the noise of consciousness,

while the tree arches above them, serene,
mottled, magnificent, Platonic, and green.

Sharon Olds

Pine Tree Ode

I was sitting on the top stones of a wall—can you
get even closer to the tree, he said, so I went
inches from the trunk of the tallest of the ones
we'd been standing among like small children
among the legs of the grown-ups.
Now, the side of my face was almost
against the bark, intimate,
I could see where its growing had pulled its surface
open, into wooden lozenges, like
stretch marks, I could not feel it breathe
but I felt it alive beside me, a huge
ant running down, and stopping, and turning
its feelers, in the air, between us, and then
walking so fast it seemed to be pouring back
up. Then I looked, up, along
the branchless stem, into the canopy,
to the needles fanning out in bunches
eating the sun. And the length of it seemed like
bravery, like strong will,
a single, whole, note, like a tenor's
cry, sustained, as if a tree were
a spurt from the earth, a heart's gush.
And the ants flowed from ground to sky,
sky to ground. I don't know where the ants
had been, or their ancestors had been, the noon
the tornado came through, wall of water
a hundred and thirty miles an hour,
solid ferocious grey static.
The tree stood. And now I sat up straight
beside it, feeling my way back
through species, and species, toward the pine, and toward
the ones we both descended from, the
fern, the green cell—the sun,
the star-stuff we are made of.

Peter Streckfus

Model of a Tree Growing in the Path of a Spiral

If a tree were to grow in a spiral path, each leaf coming only from the main trunk, the trunk traveling in a circuitous manner to maximize the area of leaf to sun's light, maintaining an equivalent mass to trees of the branching figure type, this tree would no doubt be of spherical dimensions. In order to support its own weight—once it had completed its first arches, having grown to sufficient height to lean over and touch its head to the ground: growing along the ground then for a period, until, once again, skyward and leaning over, the pliant trunk crosses itself; completing in this manner groin after groin until a sort of vault appears (a contour drawing where the instrument never leaves the marking surface)—the tree must not only cross itself over innumerable times through the span of its life, but will eventually graft to itself at these points, thereby increasing the efficiency of nutrient transport from its asymmetrically spiraling root mass (the root does not derive its energy from a single radiating source, nor need it contend with gravity in an unsupportive medium). As this network of intersecting arches we will still call a tree (its leaves appearing and disappearing with the seasons) adds cambium, layer upon layer, as the earth slides and slides on its ellipse, the spaces between this tree's junctures will diminish until, finally, the tree forms itself into a perfect hemisphere. And in the middle of this hemisphere, let there live a hen of fanned tails, and on each tail let there be an unblinking eye.

Jessica Greenbaum

The Storm-Struck Tree

As the storm-struck oak leaned closer to the house—
The remaining six-story half of the tree listing toward the glass box
Of the kitchen like someone in the first tilt of stumbling—
The other half crashed into the neighbors' yards, a colossal
Diagonal for which we had no visual cue save for
An antler dropped by a constellation—
As the ragged half leaned nearer, the second storm of cloying snow
Began pulling on the shocked, still-looming splitting, and its
     branches dragged
Lower like ripped hems it was tripping over
Until they rustled on the roof under which I
Quickly made dinner, each noise a threat from a body under which we
     so recently
Said, Thank goodness for our tree, how it has accompanied us all
     these years,
Thank goodness for its recitation of the seasons out our windows
     and over
The little lot of our yard, thank goodness for the birdsong and
     squirrel games
Which keep us from living alone, and for its proffered shade, the crack
     of the bat
Resounding through September when its dime-sized acorns
Land on the tin awning next door. Have
Mercy on us, you, the massively beautiful, now ravaged, and charged
With destruction.
We did speak like that. As if from a book of psalms
Because it took up the sky

Jennifer K. Sweeney

how to uproot a tree::

Stupidity helps.
Naiveté that your hands will undo
what does perfectly without you.
My husband and I made the decision
not to stop until the task was done,
the small anemic tree made room
for something prettier.
We'd pulled before, pale hand over wide hand,
a marriage of pulling toward us what we wanted,
pushing away what we did not.
We had a shovel which was mostly for show.
It was mostly our fingers tunneling the dirt
toward a tangle of false beginnings.
The roots were branched and bearded,
some had spurs
and one of them was wholly reptilian.
They had been where we had not
and held a knit gravity
that was not in their will to let go.
We bent the trunk to the ground and sat on it,
twisted from all angles.
How like ropes it was,
the sickly thing asserting its will
only now at the end,
blind but beyond
the idea of leaving the earth.

Elizabeth J. Coleman

Mistaking Silence for Consent

As in all towns, our oaks
wore habits of bark,

a vow of silence
taken by each tree.

Among their inhabitants
—mourning doves,

blue jays, American crow—
no unnecessary quarrel.

Just a scurrying sound,
a seed, a song.

My parents felled a tree
to build their pool,

the oak that held me,
reading, after school.

Daniel Tobin

The Tree

Where it flung itself into the sky, its canopy
of leaves darkened three lawns, branches
flaring along the power lines, out and up
to fill the block's patch of heaven,
the trunk too thick to reach arms around,
which is why it's a legend to the neighbors
who like to tell how they cut it down
before we came, after the roots grew so big
they buckled their driveway's concrete slabs,
the ground that held its wide circumference
a wispy square of grass, the great bulk vanished
like my wife's father, once tall as a film star
in her salvaged photos, or myself
a child lifting my mother, wasted drunk,
off the floor to help her into bed.
It could be anything that has a hope
of giving life, though even the stump is gone,
ground to dust by deliberate hands. Below,
the thinnest hairs still widen, mesh
together, fanning out in blind passageways
to a source: some broken seal or outflow pipe
they quietly fill and fill to convey desire
toward nothing, an absence vast as their need.
And, suddenly, you're in the basement, grabbling
through the muck and wreckage of what you thought
swept effortlessly away. You are down on your knees.

Gail Mazur

Rudy's Tree

Rudy Burckhardt, 1914-1999

I admire the way he took
   matters into his own hands
      (he didn't bring his camera

this summer—and when his son
   brought it from the city,
      never loaded it), carried

his wooden easel in from
   its station in the woods,
      the night before, no film

in his old camera, free
   of desire, the calm I imagine
      he carried with him

into the cool water,
   the early morning resolve,
      his long life behind him,

autonomous, various,
   the pond familiar.
      And now, I look into

the furrows of his painting
   hanging on my sunlit stair-
      wall in Provincetown,

the ridged bark, the deep
   fissures, gray, brown,
      black: a tree all trunk,

tree I can imagine him
  conversing with, around them
    slender new trees, green

summer ferns, a fallen pine,
  twigs, the tender lyric line
    of one luminous white

birch in the still Maine woods.
  A quiet conversation—
    like ours when we spoke

only days ago. Is it a pine?
  A hemlock? The bark
    is rough, articulate,

dense, a texture craggy
  with age. At the picture's
    heart, an inner layer, glowing.

Did I tell him that day
  how much I love living
    with it?

James Richardson

Pines

Pine—the tree, that is—grows from a root
that means to swell, from which we also get
the word *fat*, and by extension
Eire and the *Pierian* springs, for their fertility.
But the pine in *to pine for* or *to pine away*
stems from a root *to pay for* or *atone*
which gives us *penalty* and *punish* and *pain*.
Somehow two thoughts, on different sides
of a shearing fault of language, have slid together
and stuck, for our lifetimes, anyway, at the sound *pine*.

It's not so common, in this practical century,
for lovers to pine away, and as our climate warms,
pines are retreating higher, but late as it is,
anyone sleepless will hear the sound of the wind
thinning through pines as pained. Maybe at first
they were a little strange with each other,
but it's natural, now, that *pine* and *pine* are *pine*.
Just as, when two who met on a trail one morning
are still talking at sunset, something other
than matching their strides is keeping them together.

John Shoptaw

The Tree in the Midst

Long after they had lost sight of the couple
and the story that trailed after them,
the cherubim kept glaring at the horizon,
shrugging their wings at each other
and shifting their weight from fore
to hind paws. Meanwhile,
the unforbidden animals—indohyus,
field mice, Persian ground jays,
worms, salamanders, ants and so forth—
ate as always from the tree of life
and also from the tree of knowing
good fruit from fruit gone bad—
a knowledge the human animals
had picked up by watching them
from hiding. Only the Eternally
Inexperienced One had never
tried so much as a single deep ripe
pomegranate aril. It knew no more
than the cherubim that down among
the butterfly weeds the two trees
become one trunk. And so It saw to it
that the cherubim kept an eye out
for the humans, lest they lose their taste
for each other and the world, find their way
back to the pomegranate, get fed up
with living and become one of them.

Frances Richey

Ramón

Before the sores, his skin was smooth as the trunk
of a beech tree I passed every evening on my walk through
the country club across from Franklin Turnpike. In the summer,
its branches rose and fell in sweeping arcs. It was the only
tree in the yard, twenty feet from a one-story brick, like a child's
drawing, doors and windows shut. I used to wonder if anyone
lived there. If maybe the house belonged to the tree. No one
came out when I sat with my back against the bark, imagined
a picnic, friends spreading blankets. Whenever I approached,
the branches came alive, waving me back. Ramón died on a Sunday
in November. It was still raining when I returned to the world
at the edge of the stone gate—the naked bark of the beech a
darker sheen, the great trunk lengthening—

Connie Wanek

Peach Tree

She hacked a hole in the desert gravel
with her sharpened pick
and planted it last fall,
a naked stick. She was already
fonder of this brave little tree
than she'd been of any man.

When red buds finally blanketed
the spurs, she remembered her
second child, sixty years ago,
nearly dying of measles.
Then the blossoms sprang open
and swarming bees were instantly in love.

To say the tree thanked her for water
was not fanciful. Nor could she
thin the blooms. "Which?" she cried.

She'd been "put under," the way they did,
for the birth of each of her six.
Cheated, she thought now. She'd stay
until she saw peaches, real peaches.

K.A. Moon

The Oak Tree's Burden

To Clyde Johnson, lynched August 3, 1935

Your weight
bows my branch
toward the earth

I was not made for this

I will never be the same
Bent
like a fractured
           unset bone
that cannot heal straight

Gnarled the eternal nod
like your bark-colored head

So heavy
our body-breaking hour

Please
forgive me

Naomi Shihab Nye

My Father and the Figtree

For other fruits my father was indifferent.
He'd point at the cherry trees and say,
"See those? I wish they were figs."
In the evening he sat by our beds
weaving folktales like vivid little scarves.
They always involved a figtree.
Even when it didn't fit, he'd stick it in.
Once Joha was walking down the road
and he saw a figtree.
Or, later when they caught and arrested him,
his pockets were full of figs.

At age six I ate a dried fig and shrugged.
"That's not what I'm talking about!" he said,
"I'm talking about a fig straight from the earth—
gift of Allah!—on a branch so heavy it touches the ground.
I'm talking about picking the largest, fattest, sweetest fig
in the world and putting it in my mouth."
(Here he'd stop and close his eyes.)

Years passed, we lived in many houses, none had figtrees.
We had lima beans, zucchini, parsley, beets.
"Plant one!" my mother said, but my father never did.
He tended garden half-heartedly, forgot to water,
let the okra get too big.
"What a dreamer he is. Look how many things he starts
and doesn't finish."

The last time he moved, I got a phone call.
My father, in Arabic, chanting a song I'd never heard.
"What's that?" I said.
"Wait till you see!"

He took me out back to the new yard.
There, in the middle of Dallas, Texas,
a tree with the largest, fattest, sweetest figs in the world.
"It's a figtree song!" he said,
plucking his fruits like ripe tokens,
emblems, assurance
of a world that was always his own.

Cheryl Savageau

Ant Tree

This is the tree that's inhabited. I like all the little doorways, the tunneled world they live in. I travel with them into the dark heart of the tree, through the living wood, tasting the smells, hearing all the tiny feet walking steadily in. When I put a stalk of grass into the hole, ants climb out on the bridge and onto my hand. I put the stalk of grass next to them, along the side of my arm, and they obligingly climb back off. I slip the grass back into a hole in the tree so they can find their way home. Inside somewhere, I know there is a queen, fat with eggs, who smells so good these ants will not go far. I know that feeling, the good smell of my mother, my Memere, the kitchen smells of home.

Diane Seuss

[From this bench I like to call my bench I sit]

From this bench I like to call my bench I sit
and watch my tree which is not my tree, no one's
tree, the quiet! Except for barn swallows, which are
not loud birds, how many exclamation points can I
get away with in this life, who was it who said only two
or maybe seven—Bishop? Marianne Moore? Either way
the world is capable of quiet if everyone stays indoors
and no jet planes, my tree, it just stands there
in the middle of everything in a meadow on the bay
looking what Barthes called "adorable," then I drove
the mile west to the sea, which had decided to be loud
that day, the sunset, oh, ragged and bloody as a piece
of raw meat in the jaws of some big golden carnivore,
and I cried a little, for none of it! none of it will last!

Anthony Cody

Artifacts on a Hanging Tree, Goliad, Texas (a series of 70 Mexican Lynchings, 1857)

> *"Site for court sessions at various times from 1846 to 1870. Capital sentences called for by the courts were carried out immediately, by means of a rope and a convenient limb. Hangings not called for by regular courts occurred here during the 1857 "cart war"—a series of attacks made by Texas freighters against Mexican drivers along the Indianola-Goliad/San Antonian Road. About 70 men were killed, some of them on this tree, before the war was halted by Texas Rangers."*
> —State Historical Survey Committee Texas Marker near the tree

<u>Last 5 TripAdvisor Reviews of Goliad's Hanging Tree, as of 6/23/18</u>

Title: Love old court houses (6/20/18)
Review: This hanging tree was just a bonus on the court house square and the history that took place there was moving.

Title: Spooky when you think of the tree's use! (6/18/18)
Review: One of the sites in Goliad is the hanging tree a beautiful tree which was used to mete out "justice" after trials.

Title: Beauty of a tree (6/19/18)
Review: Well the name sort of says it all, but that is a beautiful tree. The courthouse is a class Texas courthouse, so the day was great.

Title: Interesting in a gruesome kind of way (5/27/18)
Review: This is a huge oak tree outside of the courthouse in Goliad. You really can picture the sentences being carried out.

Title: Huge old live oak tree (5/7/18)
Review: The tree is located in the center of town on the grounds of the county courthouse. The tree has quiet the history. When convicted, the prisoner was walked outside and hanged from this magnificent live oak tree.

Angela Narciso Torres

What Isn't There

Even without leaves
the Bradford pear keeps
its bell silhouette.

Above, a commonplace moon,
somewhere between half
and full, waxing edge

rubbed like the worn
ridges of a lucky quarter.
A sentence partly

erased—brightness
that might have been.

Natasha Trethewey

Limen

All day I've listened to the industry
of a single woodpecker, worrying the catalpa tree
just outside my window. Hard at his task,

his body is a hinge, a door knocker
to the cluttered house of memory in which
I can almost see my mother's face.

She is there, again, beyond the tree,
its slender pods and heart-shaped leaves,
hanging wet sheets on the line—each one

a thin white screen between us. So insistent
is this woodpecker, I'm sure he must be
looking for something else—not simply

the beetles and grubs inside, but some other gift
the tree might hold. All day he's been at work,
tireless, making the green hearts flutter.

Jennifer Barber

Motion Harmony #2

The pears dropped
           by the failing tree
     are pale bronze,
           sunlit with copper spots.
Rotting in the grass.
           Riddled with wasps.

By pear I mean pear,
           not a riddled heart.
     At least I think I do.
           The flesh of it laid bare
by the intricate, steady
           work of mouths.

Geraldine Zetzel

Copper Beech

Like a great fountain above
the city street it towers all summer—
massive trunk grey as a wet seal,

dark mass of limbs and leaves
looming like an August
thunder-head (though one branch

reaches out a long ungainly hand
to passers-by, as if asking to join
the lesser world).

In Spring, while other trees
leaf out in tints of green
and rose and mauve

this giant stands there, noble head
still bare. Each year in May,
I think *This time it must be dead.*

Each year, suddenly flaring
open its dark buds
again, it proves me wrong.

Calendar

Ellen Kaufman

The Cherries of Kenwood

Gaze down these pink
tunnels into deeper pink.

The walls are blossoms
fashioned of smaller blossoms

attached to raised arms
that nuzzle other arms.

It's like watching a parade
that poses while I parade.

Random sprays liven up
the trunks, remind me to look up

at where naked limbs used to be.
Where the road used to be:

melted ice cream. A girl pedals
through a puddle of petals.

Mary Jo Salter

White Petals, 3 A.M.

Lights out but it's glowing—
the dogwood's white-petaled cloud that fills
the window above the window seat
just feet from the foot of my bed.

And I'm thinking I've seen this,
the same wide-eyed whiteness, winter nights
when the naked branches were gloved in snow
that had stored the day's light somehow.

Now it's the moon
(an assumed one, out of the window's frame)
spilling light on the constellations
of blossoms, beamed through the room

to interrogate me: should people sleep
in April? The flowering out there
could be my lit-up circuitry,
my brain reflecting

on bounty. This. The moon of conscious
fullness. The brimming thing that wanes.
The tree with every fragile
petal on before the first

one falls, the sun comes up, the green
leaves take over the length of summer,
so long you forget you live in time.
Don't blink. Don't. Not again.

Peter Marcus

Dogwood Time

I wanted nothing
but to sit, and to breathe within
this white asylum,

cloistered as a sky-
blue Mary.
I'm certain if I hadn't

been at risk of arrest
for loitering, I would
have sat interminably

on the sidewalk on Perry Street,
trying to relinquish
the surges of self-pity.

But soon must come
the nails and blood
and city policemen

incorrigible,
with nightsticks and flip pads
to write summonses.

Grace Schulman

Gone

Washington Square, 2020

From my window, I see the world
without us in it: a vacant park,
a silver maple sheltering no reader;

a cherry tree dressed like a bride betrayed,
her wedding canceled; a dogwood tree
whose whites will fall without regretful eyes.

No baby strollers; no candy wrappers
stuffed in bins; just a sign, "NO bicycles,"
and memories of skateboard pirouettes.

Around us, death: the numbers spin the mind.
Fever dreams. The last breath held, alone.
I had not thought death had undone so many.

This park reminds us it was once a field
for the unclaimed dead of galloping yellow fever.
Construction workers dug up skeletons

that had lain for years beneath our footsteps.
Death in the hanging elm, a rooted gallows.
Now the clear air, pollution-free, is poison

for walkers, while trees stand stern, immune.
Sad paradox. For comfort, I recall:
Camille Pissarro would have lingered here.

He painted the Paris gardens from a window,
having left his island's sprawling shores
for tighter scenes—but he gazed at people,

matchsticks from above, in ones and twos.
Below, the park's unlittered paths are mute,
but wait: just now a mournful, prayerful sax,

unseen, from somewhere, unlooses notes,
calls me to the window, and I hear
the sounds I can't imagine days without.

Elaine Sexton

Autobiographia Literaria
after Frank O'Hara

Someday the blank page will rush
under me and with the grace

of a walk in the woods
with you, who have been silent

for years. You will blow sun
in the spring-leafed trees,

and the damp earth
will begin to dry

and crack, and the birds
who no longer migrate

will start to sing, despite
global warming, for they, too

love the author, who stumbles
through time. Still, there's a chance

that history repeating itself
will change course. *You're not*

dead yet a friend, who has
passed, liked to say, and

I've been known
to perseverate. And repeat, and repeat,

and will probably do so
from the grave, my stone

etched with the text: Not yet.

Not yet.

Toi Derricotte

Cherry Blossoms

I went down to
mingle my breath
with the breath
of the cherry blossoms.

There were photographers:
Mothers arranging their
children against
gnarled old trees;
a couple, hugging,
asks a passerby
to snap them
like that,
so that their love
will always be caught
between two friendships:
ours & the friendship
of the cherry trees.

Oh Cherry,
why can't my poems
be as beautiful?

A young woman in a fur-trimmed
coat sets a card table
with linens, candles,
a picnic basket & wine.
A father tips
a boy's wheelchair back
so he can gaze
up at a branched
heaven.
                    All around us

the blossoms
flurry down
whispering,

Be patient
you have an ancient beauty.

Be patient,
you have an ancient beauty.

Ishion Hutchinson

Moved by the Beauty of Trees

The beauty of the trees stills her;
she is stillness staring at the leaves,

still and green and keeping up the sky;
their beauty stills her and she is quiet

in her stare, her eyes' long lashes curve
and keep, her little mouth opens

and keeps still with its quiet for the beauty
of the trees, their leaves, the sky

and its blue quiet, very still and quiet;
her looking eyes wide, deep, silent

hard on the trees and the beauty
of the sky, the green of the leaves.

Rebecca Okrent

In Lieu of Flowers

The apple tree broke into blossom the morning after the school dance.
The day before girls swarmed the boys' school campus, arriving
exotic as orchids to us, faculty brats who conferred to them
our bedrooms for the night. Their femininity—spritzes
of perfume and hairspray, sliding silks and taffetas,
whispers, laughter—so pervaded our house my father
couldn't stop chuckling to himself; my mother, the care-giver,
in the kitchen regretted something, frenching the beans and
searching drawers for the garlic press.

Oh those girls were marvelous and knew things about boys
that I, surrounded as I was by them, could only imagine.
There would be secrets and kissing and dancing close.
I spent that night on the chaise in my parents' room
and woke below window-framed apple blossoms,
the tree transformed overnight into a perfumed beauty
in a gown of pinks and white. As I would one day be?
The memory, my first miracle and swooning,
cleaves like Velcro—

That's why, if I did receive flowers, I would want not lilies
with their funereal odor, nor trite gladioli or even roses,
but clouds of apple blossoms with their promise of fruit
and the transfiguration of my small life.

Rachel Hadas

Forest and Trees

Pacing the greyish green
corridor of a May
long as the slowest childhood,
I brush aside the drooping boughs to reach
a veil of intricate
and ramifying ways
to find you. Or to lose you? I forget.
Were you the habitat
through which all this cool spring
I strode? I left no stone unturned; each leaf
might signal hidden life.
I tramped up every glistening avenue,
threaded the season's maze as if
there were a destination I knew,
as if I'd reach a goal when I broke through
the stubborn undergrowth and clinging mist,
forgetting you inhabited all this,
forgetting all the greenery I so
impatiently pushed back was also you.

George Kalogeris

Veil

Caught in a sun-shower on my way to school,
I once took shelter by ducking under a willow.
Its branches hung down so low they swept the street.

I was stepping through beaded curtains, thick as catkins.
The rainwater glittered running down the vines.
My books in their slung green satchel stirred like seedlings.

Black earth. Moist roots. The bole-mouth oozing tar...
I could have waited things out in the candy store
But I was shy. I was a first-born. For years

I never knew why those elderly relatives
Would look at me that way. They spoke no English.
Their coats were heavy. Whatever they'd been through

I stepped back out from under the veil of the willow
Just as the dew was shining on everything.
The house, the sidewalk. Even the dark Atlantic.

Ted Kooser

Locust Trees in Late May

Two of them, sixty feet high, with trunks as big around
as fifty-gallon barrels, lean at a corner of the house,
sprinkling their tiny green bur-like flowers
over the deck and during windy thundershowers
dropping their sprigs of leaves, delicate as ferns.
Just weeks ago they hummed with thousands of bees,
a sound like a huge refrigerator left in the sun.

When they were young they had fierce black
two-inch thorns, but they have since grown old
along with us and have tired of defending themselves.
Just now a nuthatch flits back and forth to the feeder,
hiding sunflower seeds in the bald, wrinkled bark,
and somehow a clump of grass has taken root
in a sap-damp crotch six feet above the ground.

Autumn is still a whole summer away, but it will come,
and with it great showers of copper locust leaves
like pennies, but oval-shaped, more like those pennies
a man at a carnival many years ago rolled through
a little machine on the tailgate of his truck
that pressed the Lord's Prayer into them. Each of us
got only one, but these trees give us many.

Richard Jones

The Place des Vosges

In Jean-Paul Sartre's novel *Nausea,*
the hero's existential awakening takes place
on a bench beneath the boughs of chestnut trees
in a park much like the Place des Vosges.
Antoine Roquentin feels the cold shiver of nothingness
against the wild, unstoppable abundance of life
he found meaningless. But I find
the fountain and the branches in blossom
and this wooden bench bathed in bright sunshine
a place of perfect rest, a blessing, a gift,
and unbutton my coat to let my spirit breathe
and take flight in the afternoon breeze.
On the grass, on blankets scattered here and there,
people laze and lounge and laugh,
they have bread and wine,
they share stories about their dreams.
I'd say they haven't a care in the world
if I thought for a moment that was true,
but that is exactly what makes them beautiful,
weighty, and meaningful,
the way their joy transcends and surpasses suffering,
so that this existential moment
is something they celebrate, lifting full glasses
and, I'd like to think, remembering Sartre,
who believed in neither love nor joy
and wrote *nothingness, contingency, anguish,* and *nausea,*
though he also believed,
as I do, sitting with my pen and blue notebook
on a bench in the Place des Vosges,
in writing the *yes* of a poem.

Connie Wanek

Mulberries in the Park

At free, they're cheap
and sweet enough, and, by late July,
the tree's glad to shed them. Out there
under the storm clouds,
a slender woman reaches
into the plunging branches.
She's bridling the great green horse
in the summer pasture. She takes
a heavy bough in her arms
and feels it lift her off her feet.
She brought a dented pail
but eats as she picks, and around her
falls a shower of mulberries
from the treetop filled with starlings
as, weighted with fruit
the whole tree staggers.
Then the first raindrops tick
among the leaves. Hurry now.

Maurice Manning

The Switch

If you were going to get a switching
and told to go and cut the switch
from the switch-tree, which was a peach,
it offered the chance to study the tree,
to see the switch was bound to the branch
and with a knife you'd free the switch
which might have hurt the tree except
it quickened the tree to grow more switches,
and a lesson to learn from a number of switchings
in youth when mischief met the stare
of fury or disbelief, is switches
are stiffer after the switch-tree
has reached the end of blossom-time,
so if you didn't want the switch
to stamp itself on the back of your legs
for everyone to see and chide,
it was wise to make your mischief early
in the season, when the sap was high
and the switches hung down smooth and green
with pink blossoms promising
the switching will be smart, but brief,
and all this study of the tree
invites a catch in the throat and wonder,
because through wrong and the further wrong
on the face that showed too little regret,
there was something else you wanted to learn
and the switch was the only way to get it,
but what that was is lost, and all
there is to see in looking back
is the switch of knowledge raised to slash
the air, but just before the switching
you hear the father's voice soften,
a switching always hurts me more
than you, which is why you cut the switch.

Rick Barot

The Marrow

For a time I lived in a house with a meadow
and small woods around it. It was summer, the light

changing the meadow over the long day,
as though to illustrate the phases of consciousness:

the gold of morning, the stricken green at noon,
the shadows saturated by coolness

in the evening. Butterflies, like small yellow utility
flags, crossed the light. And the sounds

of insects and birds, little strings of notes
on staves. Deer appeared, disclosing this fact:

if you don't have hands, use your mouth.
Like clockwork, two kept coming back each morning

to the same spots, as though the grass they ate
the day before had sprung back overnight.

They were deer. Because I was not sick or in need,
they were only deer. Behind the glass

of the house, I must have been
a small distortion in the reflection they saw there,

a small motion in the surface. In the woods
were wild roses with pink edges, going white

into their centers. Under the large trees,
the ferns were a dense singularity, the span of each

frond a kind of fractal logic. I saw things
mostly as they were, which meant a kind of health.

The nights were dark, as though the house was far
inland, in the marrow of geography.

But just beyond the house and the meadow
was the ocean, which you could hear if you listened.

Cheryl Savageau

The Willow at Flint Pond

for Denise

Under the willow is where my sister and I spend the afternoon, hot in our pink and blue raincoats, while we wait for the newspapers to be delivered and the rain pours down. The air is warm and smells like places far away. I like the way it touches my cheeks, like my mother's hand the way I want it to be, soft and delicate, with the scent of roses and rain. We watch as the water collects into little streams and runs down the banking into the pond behind the willow, its edges thick in cattails ripe with fluff, carrying sticks, paper ice cream wrappers, bits of bark. Soon we are helping things along, giving things a push, blocking the water with our feet til it runs over our rubber boots. There's still no papers. The wind is blowing hard, but it's not cold. The willow bends her arms low around us, so we don't see our father when he drives by, looking for us. The wind blows our names places we can't hear. After a while, no more cars go by on the cut-off, there is just us, the wind heavy with dark and damp, as we wait under the willow.

Maxine Scates

The Orchards

There were problems to be solved then,
decisions to be made. Now we walk and walk

through the orchards, the Cannery Orchard,
the Nursery Orchard, the Black Cherry Orchard.

We walk to the river, the far boundary,
high and wide, deep and brown, a ganglia

of branches tumbling, shooting down the rapids,
then caught by the branch of a downed tree. There's

a man sitting on a bench aiming a long lens,
an old couple walking who stop to pet

our young dog. The Nursery Orchard makes me
think of how the decisions quieted, moved on,

how long ago I'd take those tests in secret,
and, never the right color, I thought it was him.

Later I found out it was both of us, and, oddly,
that made it better, our decision made. The young

trees in this orchard were grown for transplant,
or maybe they just took cuttings, because now

they're as gnarled as the tree in the meadow
they call the Wedding Tree, which was split

in a storm, its fallen branches scattered
around the still living base. It's the Goat Orchard

I keep wondering about, though—did the goats
run there the way the dogs do now

in their endless loops? Last night I saw a photo
of goats standing in the branches of a tree they climb

to eat its nuts. At first they looked much too heavy
to ride the branches, ten of them standing

in the same tree, and then they looked as light
as horned birds. So, yes, the decisions lessen

but the problems remain, the one about the heart,
the way it rises. The one about finding your way to it

as if walking in a maze of so many orchards
each one needs a name.

Don Share

Shady Grove

The heat drove me and Cleo-the-Basset
To the grace and cling of the impartial woods
Back of the clamber and blear of our street.
Like a pair of ghosts, we prowled the grove, haunted,
Worked our own private wills, green-shaded.
This was before the nation, off-stage, had the goods
On Nixon, before my ring finger was bonded gold
In wedlock, before Cleo turned blind-eyed, old.
Twists of branches and root. Dogsmell, and sweat.
The archaic slur of my accent hadn't left me yet.
Cleo and I snuffed Memphis loam like it was Heaven.
1969 was all wisdom teeth and no wisdom for me, then.

Emily Tuszynska

Floodplain

All morning in mid-labor
not ready for the hospital

          walking the floodplain

      the earth still soft
      waters receded

            tulip poplars
            knotted sycamores
            clumps of grass

ghosted with silt

the trees leaned downstream
from many floods

            I clung to them

my sisters I thought if I thought at all
somehow the term did not seem wrong

the ground was washed bare

          fibrous roots exposed

            slack water
            dusty with pollen

we walked and rested and walked again
bowing

            then kneeling

to each contraction as it came

some bright bit of blue
caught on the far bank

without panic
I felt each crest carry me farther
away from you

away from familiar ground

in the spaces between

your hands

lightly—

the air on my face—

perhaps I *was* the trees

their massive trunks shifting
as wind poured
through high branches

perhaps I was the riverbed

or the light as it pulsed between moving leaves

from all about us
a wordless insistence

deep in my interior
the forest   the water rising

Leslie Williams

In the Second Half of Life

You could make the necessary arrangements to be
walking there again, drinking from the old well
under dogwoods breaking open strong as parachutes,
to savor blossoms without fruit; you could find a small
house with a few big rooms, make a friend or two
who'd swing on the porch then fade into a comfortable
distance. You could live with an ocean view, put limpets
in a jar. You could, with no remorse, read quietly
in your room. Refuse to worry about hurting anyone.
Throw something on the fire besides yourself to cause
a merry blaze; work so everything's heightened, raised
to best translation, brightest hue; you could sleep more,
stay in touch, become a vegetarian. You could pine
for solitude and then complain of loneliness.

C. Dale Young

Cri de Coeur

The trees are dark and heavy, my love,
heavy with the sound of the locust—
the dead of summer has arrived.

The lane scripts its old questions
carefully down a canyon of trees.
Green, the sunlight shifts

and dims the credibility of things,
and then the pond is a field,
weedy and green, weedy;

the hospital, dirty squares of light
against a background of trees
dark with the sound of the locust.

Sleeping god in an age of plagues,
give us the chance to use the past tense.
Let us, with the charity of middle age, lie:

"Yes, it was all so beautiful. ..."

Robert Hass

The Problem of Describing Trees

The aspen glitters in the wind
And that delights us.

The leaf flutters, turning,
Because that motion in the heat of August
Protects its cells from drying out. Likewise the leaf
Of the cottonwood.

The gene pool threw up a wobbly stem
And the tree danced. No.
The tree capitalized.
No. There are limits to saying,
In language, what the tree did.

It is good sometimes for poetry to disenchant us.

Dance with me, dancer. Oh, I will.

Mountains, sky,
The aspen doing something in the wind.

David Ferry

October

The day was hot and entirely breathless, so
The remarkably quiet remarkably steady leaf fall
Seemed as if it had no cause at all.

The ticking sound of falling leaves was like
The ticking sound of gentle rainfall as
They gently fell on leaves already fallen,

Or as, when as they passed them in their falling,
Now and again it happened that one of them touched
One or another leaf as yet not falling,

Still clinging to the idea of being summer:
As if the leaves that were falling, but not the day,
Had read, and understood, the calendar.

Rachel Eliza Griffiths

Watching Blackbirds Turn to Ghosts

Tomoko and I talk a long time
about the gestures of a falling
leaf in autumn.

On the antenna outside
I watch a cloister of blackbirds
who are so still

they become the very shadows of blackbirds.

"The falling leaf is universal," she says
at one point.

We keep the leaf and its archetype
suspended in the air a bit longer
by talking slowly, in wonder,

while admitting it's consistently useless for us
to pretend to be clever in our poems.

I think of any leaf's shadow

going calmly to the street, beyond
the street, beyond the syntax of rot.

This morning I'd seen a woman
twisted like paper
at the bottom of a long bridge.

"Everyone will always watch leaves
fall in fall. Everyone will know this—
what it means—the simplicity

of the fall…"

Jennifer Franklin

Memento Mori: Apple Orchard

In the gold light of early October, we climb
the orchard hills searching empty trees
for apples. The boy at the gate tells us Ida Red,
Rome, Crispin, and Surprise are all ripe
and ready for our hands. We walk and walk.
The dog investigates every fallen apple
with her frantic nose. Even as we savor
the autumnal sunlight of our beginning,
headlines remind us what is lost. Large families
have picked the trees clean, leaving plastic
bottles and paper napkins blowing like white flags.
Instead of the fragrant apples on the ground
reminding me of my mother's baking,
I catch the smell of decay.

I catch the smell of decay
as we walk through so many rows
of stubby trees that we cannot find our way
back to the car. We do not say what we're thinking—
if we leave without a single apple, it might mean
what we have done to the earth cannot be undone.
The children who grow up on this imperiled planet
will not remember pulling the russet fruit
from the branches to bite into its sweet flesh. We see
boys throw bruised apples at each other. Still children,
they already know what is damaged becomes a weapon.
As we pull away, we watch them run the worn paths.
Their masks fall as they bend to collect
the blemished apples and fill their empty bags.

Robert Hedin

Monarchs, Viceroys, Swallowtails

For years they came tacking in, full sail,
Riding the light down through the trees,
Over the rooftops, and not just monarchs,
But viceroys, swallowtails, so many
They became unremarkable, showing up
As they did whether we noticed them or not,
Swooping and fanning out at the bright
Margins of the day. So how did we know
Until it was too late, until they quit coming,
That the flowers in the flowerbeds
Would close their shutters, and the birds
Grow so dull they'd lose the power to sing,
And how later, after the river died,
Others would follow, admirals, buckeyes,
All going off in some lavish parade
Into the great overcrowded silence.
And no one bothered to tell the trees
They wouldn't be coming back any more,
The huge shade trees where they used
To gather, every last branch and leaf sagging
Under the bright freight of their wings.

John Koethe

Burnished Days

> I came back at last to my own house.

I went for a walk this afternoon,
Down Mercer Street, past the Seminary
And out to the Graduate College, revisiting
The world where I began to feel like this
And sound this way. I clambered up the carillon
To see the local world, and wandered through the arch
Where Willy used to hear his family's voices.
We like to think that we're the logical conclusion
Of what we knew, and the choices we made,
But it isn't true. I think "But it isn't true"
Should be my motto, or the fortune in my cookie,
For whatever the book of the past contains
I don't know how to read it. The certainties of a day
Give way to second thoughts and doubts, and questions
Come quickly, to which the answers take their time.
The January sun was filtering through the trees
As I walked back home, subdued by the second sight
Of bare branches intertwined with evergreens and yellow
Sunlight on the towers, as the light declined.

Ed Ochester

Fall

Crows, crows, crows, crows
then the slow flapaway over the hill
and the dead oak is naked

Jennifer Markell

Leaf Litter

Tomorrow my father will lie down
with flowers. All summer I've searched
the canopy, looking for something.
Sometimes I think I see it

but then the wind.
The sycamore sheds untimely
litter, August leaves moldering
with prodigal marigolds.

Lace-wing flies dip into hedges,
lift over lonely kitchens,
hospital rooms exhausted with dreams.
I sit with a thin washcloth

wiping my father's forehead,
hold the hand that's not his hand.
Nurses flit like shadows in reverse.
Crickets chip the dark.

Poppies in a vase, un-swayed,
stoic as children building
oak leaf fortresses in the street,
cars barreling through.

Early this morning, sweeping leaves,
the call came from the hospital:
Come now if you want to see him.

Major Jackson

Thinking of Frost

I thought by now my reverence would have waned,
matured to the tempered silence of the bookish or revealed
how blasé I've grown with age, but the unrestrained
joy I feel when a black skein of geese voyages like a dropped
string from God, slowly shifting and soaring, when the decayed
apples of an orchard amass beneath its trees like Eve's
first party, when driving and the road Vanna-Whites its crops
of corn whose stalks will soon give way to a harvester's blade
and turn the land to a man's unruly face, makes me believe
I will never soothe the pagan in me, nor exhibit the propriety
of the polite. After a few moons, I'm loud this time of year,
unseemly as a chevron of honking. I'm fire in the leaves,
obstreperous as a New England farmer. I see fear
in the eyes of his children. They walk home from school,
as evening falls like an advancing trickle of bats, the sky
pungent as bounty in chimney smoke. I read the scowl
below the smiles of parents at my son's soccer game, their agitation,
the figure of wind yellow leaves make of quaking aspens.

Alicia Suskin Ostriker

October; November

October

Our elegant Japanese maple
stands in a pool of rubies
or dried blood

like a dancer
who has just received
the biopsy report from the lab

and for a moment thinks
how can this be happening to me
I did everything right

November

Still a few glorious flying amber leaves
but the winter dark is rising
the grass withered the cones broken

when I think of the countless seeds
wasted by every tree every year
the way each life produces so much death

is a sort of agony and still each seed
down in the dirt is gambling or voting
hoping each November for the best

Afaa Michael Weaver

Leaves

The lines that make you are infinite, but I count them
every day to hear the stories you carry. These are not secrets
but records, things we should know but ignore. If I commit
the sin of tearing you from the tree, I find another world
inside the torn vein, another lifetime of counting the records
of who walked here before, of what lovers lay here
holding each other through wars and starvation.

Some days I stand here until I lose focus and travel,
drifting off out of the moment, too full of it, and my legs
are now like trees, mindless but vigilant, held
into the earth by the rules of debt, what we owe
to nature for trying to tear ourselves away. I drift
and the pleasure of touch comes again, layers of green
in the mountainside a tickling in my palms.

The pleasure is that of being lost here in the crowd
of trunks and pulp, the ground thick with the death of you,
sinking under my feet as I go, touching one and another,
linking myself through until the place where I entered
is gone. When I am afraid, my breath is caught in my throat.
When I am not afraid, I lift both hands up under a bunch
of you to find the way the world felt on the first day.

Alan Feldman

In November

When my daughter calls
and I can hear her baby
crying in the back seat
and she asks, "Dad, would you mind if I stop by
for a quick diaper change and feeding?"—

I'm so glad I picked up the phone,
glad I hadn't set off on my walk,
and quite soon I see her car rolling into the driveway,
and the baby is stretching open her little mouth
and wailing, as babies do—
so enraged not to be able to speak,
not even to be able to think this or that is wrong
except that the whole universe is wrong.

And when they're settled in the little bedroom off the kitchen,
and the baby is sucking noisily,
and then, contented once more,
rolling both eyes, not always in the same direction—
mother and baby in the bedroom
where my daughter herself was once diapered and fed—

I feel so thankful for never having strayed very far
into the wide world, never having served
in the foreign wars of my time, and grief for fathers
who do, the ones swaddled in flags—
maybe because yesterday was Veterans Day,
and though she says she's never done this before,
my daughter tells me she called up a soldier's family she knew
just to say she'd been thinking of them, just hoping
the war we have now will end soon.

And the thin November light is straining through the window curtains
we've never changed,
and I feel thankful for my years right here in this house
the way I imagine a tree might feel thankful
if it were ever given an opportunity to roam around the world—

how it might say, "So good of you, but no thank you,
where would the birds be without me here?—
the ones that fly back unpredictably
to perch in my thinning hair,
this and every November."

Robin Becker

The Grief of Trees

1

We returned at night, all the autumn trees
frozen beneath white crust. In the dark
we kicked at lilac boughs, Japanese maples,

and the rounded limbs sprang back.
We kicked and unfastened the stooped limbs
of the chestnut tree from a tent of snow.

And we struck the buried
laurel bushes to which the leaves still clung,
and we punted ice from tiny pines.

And from the shed she drew a spade
and worked her way around the perimeter
of the place and hacked at the heavy sacks

of wet snow wedged in the brimming branches.
Above her, the splintered shafts of spruce and fir;
before her, a hundred severed limbs her length

dented the insolent ice. I imagined that she could drop
each broken branch into a carafe of water,
and like ivy, each would grow a transparent root.

2

The next day Beth brought her chain saw
and five friends hauled sawed-off limbs to the road.
Beth saved her birch trees, staying up all night

to beat them with a broom, while transformers blew.
The worst part, she said, was the sound
of breaking leads, the wheeze before the crack,

the quick snap of the smaller branches
and the aching refrain
of trunks that slowly opened and split.

Along the village streets and rural roads—
storied heaps of dismembered oak and elm
deployed for cordwood, the grief of trees.

You pour forty pounds of birdseed into the barrel
and check the feeders. While we were away, a neighbor
kept them full, and that first morning you woke

to find junco and titmouse and nuthatch and cardinal
and a new bird feeding above the devastation,
the evening grosbeak, like the storm, just passing through.

Carol Light

Downdraft

The deer dislike the lavender and heather.
Beyond the lattice fence, a buck browses
the youngest of the apple trees. The fig
swabs bedroom windows with its splashy leaves.
As if to hector the roses, pruned and mulched,
as if they've forgotten November, a scrawny pair
of poppies bristle and clench, too orange, too red:
thumbs in the eye of the weather. And a crow
plucks lumps of pumpkin from the compost bin.
I dry my boots beside the fire. I set
my tea to steep on the ledge. The dog's asleep
beneath my elbow. Warm as toast and snug,
smug as some tweedy squire, I survey
the possibilities. Who wouldn't stop
to watch those antlers strop? Who's never been
the thrashed sapling or brazen bud,
all thin dignity determined to arrive?
A gust pipes the chimney, fipple and chiff,
with a rasping hum, and a hum, and a downdraft
puffs once. Crow and pumpkin: yet to come.

Esther Lin

Winter

In order to see my first
pear tree

I took three trains

to a cloister shipped stone by stone
from Spain to Washington Heights,

then reconstructed to a more perfect whole
enclosing

gardens laid by scholars of tapestry
and stained-glass and the poetry of flowers,
treatises on horticultural virtue,

and inside one of these
a tree.

~

Not knowing cold
my brother was seized
when he stepped from the plane.

Once an ice-pop
shared among three

cold could be laid on the kitchen board
and cut carefully by our father—we watched

carefully—into equal pieces
to place in our mouths and suck.

~

With my husband
I wanted to be as children,
sex a discovery
we could publish, win scientific prizes
for—I stroked his nipple to make it true,
true as children making their way
through a house
until someone bled,
someone got angry and then
we tiptoed.

~

Before he died
my father said
what no one wished to hear.

We should have stayed.

~

In place of marble
we weighed stone pine and magnolia,

the difference being *the stone pine
is native to Italy, Lebanon, and Syria*

and *the magnolia evolved*

*before the appearance
of bees* and my brother stood between

two planters, speckled
in their shade, saying over and over,
                              I don't know.

They both feel like him, to me.

Listening, Telling

Jericho Brown

The Trees

In my front yard live three crepe myrtles, crying trees
We once called them, not the shadiest but soothing
During a break from work in the heat, their cool sweat

Falling into us. I don't want to make more of it.
I'd like to let these spindly things be
Since my gift for transformation here proves

Useless now that I know everyone moves the same
Whether moving in tears or moving
To punch my face. A crepe myrtle is

A crepe myrtle. Three is a family. It is winter. They are bare.
It's not that I love them
Every day. It's that I love them anyway.

Sheila Black

Corona (1)

In half-empty Colorado Springs,
we are thinking about trees,
which have no choice about not
moving, while shelves empty as people
hoard things they are not sure
they will need. The aspens are yellow
from winter; the spring will be late
this year. I will take nothing from
this place but a handful of dried
cherries. An image of my daughter
kicking wet leaves. We speak too much of
what the aura of danger might be,
if we can see it or not, if we can feel
a sickness spreading before it
arrives. We speak of how each year
we miss the day in autumn when
the aspen shudders slightly and
the leaves fall all at once. Their time
different than ours; we have never
even caught the moment of their
blooming. Will our quarantine
from the loud noise of our lives
help us see inside? I crowd myself
with visions meant to comfort me
in which I drink their sap with my children,
my mouth dripping with a
cold gold, gold of crowns, the light
around a moon or minor planet
that makes it seem so much
more than it is.

Khaled Mattawa

My City

And now to my disheveled city, which lit up in rebellion, then turned on itself with assassinations and riots leading to outright war. Downtown, with its date-palm-frond-covered souqs and its charming worn-out piazzas, where I spent much of my childhood, became the battleground. Combatants fought alley to alley, house to house, room to room, exactly as the dictator they'd toppled foretold. As the fighting spread and intensified, civilians scurried to the outskirts, regrouped in clans, armed themselves to scavenge the failing state's remains. The city, built on drained marshland, became a vista of ruin and conflagration, interrupted now and then by shimmering lagoons formed from the broken sewer system and seawater overflow. The fighting has ended, but the ruins will likely remain for a long time to come. As I watch the footage now, I notice reeds several feet high, young date palms and eager eucalyptus trees rising among the rubble of bombed-out modern towers and squat mud-walled homes.

A scruffy opulence
veils the ruins green. Nests
and birdsong to soothe

the mind's exhausted surf. Trees
can console.
But not enough.

Linda Pastan

Vertical

Perhaps the purpose
of leaves is to conceal
the verticality
of trees
which we notice
in December
as if for the first time:
row after row
of dark forms
yearning upwards.
And since we will be
horizontal ourselves
for so long,
let us now honor
the gods
of the vertical:
stalks of wheat
which to the ant
must seem as high
as these trees do to us,
silos and
telephone poles,
stalagmites
and skyscrapers.
But most of all
these winter oaks,
these soft-fleshed poplars,
this birch
whose bark is like
roughened skin
against which I lean
my chilled head,
not ready
to lie down.

Charles Coe

Mulberries

One day near the end of summer vacation
when all the easily picked berries had been plundered,
a few buddies and I climbed the tallest mulberry tree
in Military Park on a dare, to the highest branches
that would support our weight, and lying back
on sturdy limbs, lounging like young lords,
reached out to pluck those darkest berries
beyond the reach of earthbound peasants,
our only competition the indignant birds
who complained at our intrusion before flying off.

With machine-like efficiency we dispatched
those berries bursting with juice that dyed our lips
and tongues and teeth purple and ran down our chins.
Eating our fill, beyond our fill, we finally slowed,
leaning back on our thrones in the sky.

Down on the ground the world carried on
in the usual way. There was the distant cry of a baby
in a carriage, the rumble of a truck, like muted thunder.

And all the while, creeping up like a slow-moving fog,
the inevitability of sixth grade, of starched nuns
and math homework, and one more step toward distant,
unimaginable adulthood. We had no words
for any of this. We just felt it in our muscles, our bones.

As golden light filtered through the leaves
and late afternoon melted into early evening,
we knew our mothers stood on porches and back stoops,
waiting to call us to the suppers for which we now had no room.

The hard branches had begun to punish our backs
and the rough bark chafe our skin, so on some silent signal,
like birds changing course midflight, we began our descent,
coming down more carefully than we'd climbed,
returning reluctantly to the ordinary world.

Stephanie Burt

Callimachus, Iamb 4, frag. 194

Εἷς—οὐ γάρ;—ἡμέων, παῖ Χαριτάδεω, καὶ σύ

Once on the hill of Tmolus
a laurel tree and an olive got into a fight,
    or rather the laurel decided to pick on the olive,
making a kind of susurrus with her new leaves
    to get the older tree's attention,
then launching in.
    "What house lacks me" (she said)
"across its lintel,
    what priest of Apollo refuses to carry me?
The Pythian oracle reclines
    on beds of my feuilletons,
and sets me on fire in order to see what she sees.
    With Phoebus on my side I took away
the plague in Ionia. My fumes fit magic spells.
    Worshippers raise me up in their round dance;
athletes and singers crave me as their prize,
    and I am carried to Delphi in holy procession.
I am so holy that I am not allowed
    to approach sites of mourning and of sorrow;
nobody wants to leave me in a grave,
    whereas your wood, lowly olive,
is something to burn at funerals."

    The laurel's oily rival
responded right away: "My lovely friend,
    my swan, my wondrous, peerless,
gorgeous one, you don't understand.
    At all. No honor is greater
than to go with the dead,
    the casualties of battle,
white-haired ladies and men,
    and all the others for whom
I witness their passage out of this life; my twigs

snap with pride over any path
that pallbearers and mourners choose to walk.
     There is no holier sound
than that percussive music.
     Better this role alone
than to be some game's prize.
     That said, I am also a prize,
the one given in the Olympic
     Games, a higher place
than anything Delphi holds.
     I am not, however, given
to the loquacious, the versifying boasters
     for their amplitudinous ornamentation.
I'd rather shut up and listen." But then two doves
     who nest in the olive's branches spoke up: one asked,
"Who made the laurel? Who created the olive?"
     "What about the grape, the oak, the fir?"
"Pallas Athena made the olive: that's
     how she became patron of Athens,
winning her contest against the god of salt water."
     "But divine Apollo made the laurel.
Comparing origins isn't going to help."
     "What can you do with the berries that grow on laurel?
You can't eat them, or drink them, or even make jewelry.
     Olives, on the other hand…there's oil,
and tapenade, and pickling, and so much—
     they can even be used as solid measures,
or baked into something like bread in emergencies.
     As for Apollo, it was the curve of the olive's
trunk that gave much-needed rest
     to his mother and the mother of Artemis,
generous, vexed, long-hidden Leto."
                "We have a winner."
The laurel shook. The olive let the wind
keep moving around her knotty trunk, at her own pace.
     Then a rosebush spoke up, or rather
had barely begun to speak, with her scratchy throat

that took so long to clear, when the laurel
cut in: "You have no right
to start comparing yourself to either of us.
You're not on our level. You've never been
the gift of any god,
and when you try to speak, it's like burps in brass,
far away, mixed with grunts and scrapes and baas."
But the olive let
the wind move at her own pace,
and seemed to tilt a low branch toward the earth,
and both the doves turned back to their small nest.

It Begins with the Trees

Two full cypress trees in the clearing
intertwine in a way that almost makes

them seem like one. Until at a certain angle
from the blue blow-up pool I bought

this summer to save my life, I see it
is not one tree, but two, and they are

kissing. They are kissing so tenderly
it feels rude to watch, one hand

on the other's shoulder, another
in the other's branches, like hair.

When did kissing become so
dangerous? Or was it always so?

That illicit kiss in the bathroom
of the Four-Faced Liar, a bar

named after a clock, what was her
name? Or the first one with you

on the corner of Metropolitan
Avenue, before you came home

with me forever. I watch those green
trees now and it feels libidinous.

I want them to go on kissing, without
fear. I want to watch them and not

feel so abandoned by hands. Come
home. Everything is begging you.

Robert Cording

At the Cemetery

After my son's death October leaves fell
on schedule. Wood smoke blew across a field.

I could find nothing to steer the days.
There was only the lifeless freedom

of my own helplessness. My future seemed
unendurable, and yet it had to be endured.

Now, I meet him at his grave.
He is dead, but his death is still living.

A summer thunderstorm announces itself
in flashes and gusts of wind that rip leaves

from the maple tree beside his grave.
Beside his grave, again I think of his birth.

Unplanned, at home, ten minutes from first pains
to his being here. Just like that, I feel him

rushing into my hands, the weight of him.
I think of this so I do not lose my fatherhood.

Now, as trees bend south to north in the cemetery,
and the storm approaches, *groaning* as St. Paul

says the world groans like a mother in childbirth,
I groan: Lord, grant me this fatherhood of pain,

do not let grief be finished with me,
if only because it gives birth to my dead son

who is both not here, and not not here.

Leslie Harrison

[Parable]

I wake and once again the trees have come the trees

have once again grown through me in sleep a tiny forest

tiny tangled copse come to populate all the windswept

all the empty spaces dendritic roots curl around cells

as if around stones and the furling tender leaves their

hungry wait for light and now the trees fill with birds

whose wings I feel as faint capillary flutter whose songs

rustle in the blood autumn now and the leaves loosen

begin their fall the tiny spiders move in set about their

careful work stitching leaves back to branches mending

the quilted sky the geese travel over and in the woods

the mist descends everything is indistinct bleached and

pale the mist tastes in the muscles the throat like a chill

when the mist dissipates it takes everything with it

branches leaves spiders their sticky useless sutures

even the trees are gone the spaces full of snow and now

the snow too is gone the spaces are meadows again

are empty again and now this is who is what I am

Patricia Clark

The Canopy

In truth, Cloverdale Road doesn't end, blacktop
    giving way to packed Michigan dirt,
        dark brown, unrutted, and the car's
    tires keep humming, it's just the tune
        riffing, something I listen for.
           The trees all dripping.

Come spring, the waited-for season, the woods
    reveal their true business, layer welcoming
        the next, as first the forest floor
    blooms, then subsequent layers, bush,
        small sapling, up and up to
           white oak, American beech.

They call wildflowers that come back
    spring ephemerals. Their time of bloom
        in sequence before the canopy
    closes, dark, impenetrable.
        The list grows long—wood anemone,
           blue cohosh, great waterleaf—

on and on, in columns, alphabetical, not listed
    by common name but by family.
        Thus, the anemone group.
    Blue cohosh joins the caulophylum
        members. No surprise that waterleaf, both
        Virginianum and the great,

belong to the hydrophyllum group.
    Today, driving through downpours, rain
        lashing at times, and now, walking,
    I note how brief the time allowed for them,
        for us, light, air, vertical space to thrive in,
        before the canopy closes.

Lynn Domina

Alleluia

Apples tempt the orchard keeper to praise
binges of heat, blustery light, seasonal frost, so he grafts Gala to
    Ambrosia,
calling his hybrid Alleluia. Solid buds, pink blossoms tinged with cream,
drooping and fallen petals lead to Alleluia. He's usually reserved,
easy in silence, in evening stillness and hushed dawn. During spring,
    he listens
for crickets and bullfrogs belching praise of themselves, their own
great bellies, their unending wakefulness. He believes he hears
honeybees fertilizing his Alleluia, their faithful hum stoking his
imagination, his conviction—bees delight in joyous pollen.
    Couldn't fantasy be
juxtaposed with fact, everything a bold hybrid, orchards and orchard
keepers, blossoms and fruit, beetles and blight leaping from God's
    own mind, every
last creature chanting Alleluia. Lately, he hopes God's appetite grows
marvelously, God's desire expansive and anticipant. You surely
never imagined such variety, he whispers, peeling spirals of red skin.
    He juices
overripe Braeburns. He bakes apple strudel, dumplings, apple walnut
pie, every serving rich with cinnamon and nutmeg, sweet with cream.
Quince seeds quickened to life in mulched earth, their brambly twigs
resurrected every June, bursting with fruit by fall, false apples he admits,
seldom shapely or quite ripe, but quince jelly quavers and glistens,
translucent and brimming with secret praise. His own praise
ushers in mornings damp with fog, hums through humid afternoons,
    raucous as God's own
voice, lyrical as God's own command: let creation be
without limit, let abundance burst from Baldwin, Jonathan, Golden
    Delicious. Let wind soften to
xylophonic breeze, leaf skittering against leaf, limbs arced with
    fruit,
yellow and red and green, sweet, tart, crisp, every apple
zealous with praise, fervent with song, singing, yes, say it, Alleluia.

Gretchen Marquette

What I've Learned about Cottonwoods

(I)

The body has deep fissures.
It doesn't dry well. It rots,
splits poorly.

(II)

Cottonwood is a *riparian* tree,
which pertains to rivers. The word *arrive*
originally meant *to touch the shore* as in a boat
onto the bank of a river. It's too late to tell you,
but I think you'd have liked to know—

(III)

A cottonwood's heart-shaped leaves
are the favored food of the larva
of Banded Wooly Bears. Hatching in autumn,
they spend the winter frozen.
First its heart stops, then its gut freezes,
then its blood. Were you ever listening?
I want you to listen now.

(IV)

A cottonwood's serrated leaves
split wind from light. We lie
in our bedroom shaped
like a boxcar and listen
to the cottonwood's
absentminded
rending.

(V)

The white tufts. A small child comes
into the yard, touches them, tentatively.
I think about touching our own child that way.
Imagine us, making something new in our old world.
Something that leaves a print. In Italy, they call them
flowers of the people. In Minnesota, children
pretend they're snow.

(VI)

Paste a leaf of cottonwood
on each temple and wait until it falls
on its accord, you will be cured. The word
accord comes from Latin and meant
to bring to heart.

(VII)

When the wind stopped, I walked into the park
to see about the cottonwood. The leaves
were torn and scattered. Fresh leaves
steeped in cold, believed to purify the blood,
to heal an inflamed heart. Upside down
against wet grass, they were the wrong
kind of green. The tree itself
was unmoved.

Brian Turner

Eulogy

It happens on a Monday, at 11:20 a.m.,
as tower guards eat sandwiches
and seagulls drift by on the Tigris river.
Prisoners tilt their heads to the west
though burlap sacks and duct tape blind them.
The sound reverberates down concertina coils
the way piano wire thrums when given slack.
And it happens like this, on a blue day of sun,
when Private Miller pulls the trigger
to take brass and fire into his mouth.
The sound lifts the birds up off the water,
a mongoose pauses under the orange trees,
and nothing can stop it now, no matter what
blur of motion surrounds him, no matter what voices
crackle over the radio in static confusion,
because if only for this moment the earth is stilled,
and Private Miller has found what low hush there is
down in the eucalyptus shade, there by the river.

Howard Schwartz

Ari in the Forest

Child
of my child,
I take you for a walk in the forest.
Your hand in mine,
I feel like a creator
as I reveal this world
of shadows and light
to you.

Nothing in your experience
of rooms and parks
has prepared you
for this unbounded place.
But you take it all in stride,
following the forest path
wherever it goes.

Resting on a log,
you peer into the branches,
seeing the world with the new eyes
I long for.
I, like you,
came here
from a place of darkness
and made it my home.

Martha Collins

from *Blue Front*

There were trees on those streets that were named
for trees: Sycamore, Cedar, Poplar, Pine,
Elm, where the woman's body was found,
where the man's body was taken and burned—

There must have been trees, there were trees
on Seventh Street, in front of the house that stands
in the picture behind the carriage that holds
the boy's mother, the boy's cousin, the boy—

And of course there were trees on Washington
Avenue, wide boulevard lined with exotic
ginkgoes, stately magnolias, there were trees
on that street that are still on that street,

trees that shaded the fenced-in yards of the large
Victorian houses, the mansion built by the man
who sold flour to Grant for the Union troops,
trees that were known to the crowd that saw

the victim hanged, though not on a tree, this
was not the country, they used a steel arch
with electric lights, and later a lamppost, this
was a modern event, the trees were not involved.

Jacquelyn Pope

Trespass

The forest preserved is a flood plain
depending from the road,

the river run out of rights, resorted
to a trace. On either bank

humps of felled trees sorted
into stacks: oak and elm and ash,

the interceding pine,
remaindered but still round

and somehow whole, in this,
the gap of days before their

trunks and limbs and leaves
will be ground to chips and dust,

when the crown of their absence
is still legible. Sun sheds

through the new cut of sky.
Sparrow, squirrel and owl once

again unhomed. With each repeated
theft of shelter, filter, shadow

by eminent domain the only
domains left are pockets, parcels, scraps

and vacancies. Someday even mud
and stone will go gasping for breath.

Kim Stafford

Lessons from a Tree

Seed split. Root sprout. Leaf bud.
Delve deep. Hold fast. Reach far.
Sway. Lean. Bow. Loom.

Climb high. Stand tall. Last long.
Grow. Thicken. Billow. Shade. Sow seed.

Rise by pluck, child of luck,
lightning-struck survivor.

Burn. Bleed. Heal. Remember. Testify.
Nest. Host. Guard. Honor.

Fall. Settle. Slump.
Surrender. Offer. Enrich.

Be duff. Enough.

Frances McCue

Cedar Theater

Through the curtain of trees,
we traveled to the stage.
The land was cut to clear
along the angles bladed

while the plight of rain
dipped the slope askew.
We came into the terrain
of the timber room.

A lidless place, but for fog.
Miles out, the squalling
sea froth smudged on bights:
a red boat tipping in the trawl.

The forest, upended there,
was a lumber-scree
unleashed, a run of snared,
disheveled ghost trees:

roots cut from the upper
growth braided in the gnarl,
while the wind's brush shuddered
through the dirt and snarl.

The way a lumberman
might wrap his coat and sniff
the air, we took the span
and held it in; the whiff

of bark once spat by saws
now lifted off into trucks.
We turned and left, but paused
for all the timber shucked

and tossed to freight. Our other
clear-cut formed a stage,
one planked and covered
indoors: a theater made

from timber in the core
of our city. We lined
the stage and unfurled
a curtain, the plot unmined

until the verse took hold
when the poets came,
stepping into folds
of the velvets, timber-tamed.

Sharon Olds

New England Camping Ode

We're driving through a state forest,
he says it would take a summer—from last
frost, to first frost—to walk
the Appalachian Trail. You would mail yourself
two-week packets of dried food
to a dozen small-town post offices...
And I think, for a minute, what it would be like
to wake at first light, and go to your little
hand-dug latrine—after some months,
the dirt-filled pits like the dotted line behind
Vasco da Gama's ship on the map—then add
sticks to the coals for the new day's fire, and boil
water for coffee, pack in a dozen
sugar cubes, for each day,
168 for two weeks,
box like a building made of rough bright rooms,
then strike camp, and walk among
the ancestors. For a moment, I imagine
that journey of a summer. And then I wonder, how
much of the fear which many women
have of dangerous men in the woods
do many men have of dangerous
men in the woods. Half? A quarter?
An eighth of a teaspoon? And how much of our fear is that
during the rape, we know that he is likely
to kill us when he's done. Forgive me, pines and
beeches, hemlocks and larches, forgive me
branches, leaves, needles, cones,
spiders' webs, lichens, nests,
dragonfly camping out
in the air, his food stored in it,
forgive me, damselfly, beating her
wings in the web, suddenly soaring

out, forgive me for speaking of such scenes
here in your home of forage and order
I may not, for my fearful nature,
enter, for a summer.

Arthur Sze

The Radiant's

the origin point of a meteor shower.
      Peaches redden: branches
            are propped with juniper posts

and a shovel; steam rises
      from a caldera; stepping
            through a lava tube, we emerge

into a rain forest dotted
      with wild ginger; desire
            branches like mycelium.

Carrying a bolete in a basket,
      we forage under spruce and fir
            in cool alpine air;

a plume rises where lava reaches
      the ocean. Who said, *Out of nothing*
            nothing can come? We do not lie

in a meadow to view the Perseids
      but discover, behind a motel,
            a vineyard, and gather as we go.

Marsha Pomerantz

Not Pigment, Not Truth

Cézanne, "A Bend in the Forest Road"

Only a place
to lay down
face up
side by side
a life's
short lines,
stroke
by stroke,
and see if
they reach:

a corduroy road
over which
burdens of light
clatter into a
possible moment,
jarring
the traveler
trunk and
limb.

Stephen Ackerman

Under the Linden

You stroll through the Brandenburg Gate
On your holiday,
Under the weight of history—
Napoleon and the Storm Troops
And the revolutionaries of 1848.

And did this linden tree hear Hitler's oratory?
Is this little leaf a National Socialist
Or a pacifist?
You say, it's part of the resistance,
Part of the world's appalling beauty.

Jessica Goodfellow

Humans Naming Trees
after a line from Tristan Tzara

willow, sallow, blackthorn
thought is made in the mouth

quaking aspen, silver birch
pulse is mouth in the wrist

cedar, alder, slippery elm
wrist is grief in the making

camphor, blue ash, blister fir
myth is spindrift of grief

hawthorn, hemlock, paper birch
makeshift myth in the named

linden, rowan, tamarack
name: oh torque of the tongue

red spruce, torch pine, slash pine
pine, pine, pine, pulse, pine

Deborah Leipziger

Lobo

For Lobo, Guardian of the Amazon, killed by illegal loggers

I guard the forest
its canopy of reflected stars
the morpho butterflies   the blue moons
bromelias   the fish
the roots of trees
   drinking in the river

I guard the forest
the children of the tribe

I guard the canopy with its toucans   parakeets
emerald
I guard the forest floor   with its snakes
I guard the mating jaguars

I knew
they would kill me.
I could not have imagined
that it would be a shot to the
face   that my body would be
left in the forest

Now
You guard the forest
its canopy of reflected stars
the morpho butterflies   the blue moons
bromelias   the fish
the roots of trees
   drinking in the river

You guard the forest
the children of the tribe

You guard the canopy with its toucans   parakeets
emerald
You guard the forest floor   with its snakes
You guard the mating jaguars

Valencia Robin

Cathedral

Not that I needed reminding, but even the trees, the trees!
Like giant awestruck afros grown in the laboratory
of a mad brother, the nerdy Nerudian of my dreams
who's somehow isolated the colors of all the saddest love songs

in the world—*Baby, baby red* and *Please, please, please*
yellow, yes, even the browns are talking to me, the greens
blue in this early autumn light that makes everything shout.
And where's my hopeless agnostic when I need her,

foreseer of endless wars and sorrows? Is that her running
toward that old abandoned church, cathedral of shadow
and grass? The leaves above trembling like tambourines,
two happy squirrels dancing down the aisle.

Linda Zisquit

more desirable than gold [Psalm 19]

He spoke after love of honey.
The sun that shone behind him
blazed around us
though we were in shadow.
A bee dozed by.
If there is suffering there is also memory.
I cannot forget the moment of his breath
or the light around his face,
a tree rustling,
pebbles stirring beneath us.
He said tomorrow and meant yesterday.
Gold becomes dim in the eyes
of the tired, the fire ceases to rage.
There is no utterance, there are no words
whose sound goes unheard:
speech of tree and whisper of stone.
Only the sun still burns
with a glint of his gaze.

Erica Funkhouser

from Pome: *Malus domestica*

Bell's Early
Warren Russet
Red Gilliflower
Chenango
Black Oxford
Sops of Wine
Northern Spy
Crow Egg
Sweet Greening
Red Streak
Roman Stem
Antonovka
Blue Pearmain
Baldwin
Nodhead
Mollywopper
Roxbury Russet
Quince of Cole
Aunt Hannah
Yellow Transparent
Doctor Brooks
Back-Door Sweet
Silken Leaf
Smokehouse
Nonesuch
Summer Paradise
Opalescent
Vandevere
Crowninshield Sweet
Sweet Janet
Astrachan
Fameuse
Autumn Strawberry

Ben Davis
Cox's Orange Pippin
Rome Beauty
Sheep's Snout
Gravenstein
Fallawater
Winter Stripe
Evening Party

Joy Harjo

Speaking Tree

I had a beautiful dream I was dancing with a tree.
—Sandra Cisneros

Some things on this earth are unspeakable:
Genealogy of the broken—
A shy wind threading leaves after a massacre,
Or the smell of coffee and no one there—

Some humans say trees are not sentient beings,
But they do not understand poetry—

Nor can they hear the singing of trees when they are fed by
Wind, or water music—
Or hear their cries of anguish when they are broken and bereft—

Now I am a woman longing to be a tree, planted in a moist, dark earth
Between sunrise and sunset—

I cannot walk through all realms—
I carry a yearning I cannot bear alone in the dark—

What shall I do with all this heartache?

The deepest-rooted dream of a tree is to walk
Even just a little ways, from the place next to the doorway—
To the edge of the river of life, and drink—

I have heard trees talking, long after the sun has gone down:

Imagine what would it be like to dance close together
In this land of water and knowledge...

To drink deep what is undrinkable.

Jeffrey Harrison

Thinning the Spruces

I've become ruthless with the spruces
that crowd the hillside between the cabins and the lake,
filling every available space and leaving no room
for the slower growing maples and birches.
I yank the little ones up by the roots
and get down on my knees to cut
the trunks of the larger ones with a handsaw.
Soon I'm covered with sweat, needles, and dirt,
and my wrists, between my cuffs and work gloves,
are flecked with blood. Anyone watching me
might think I hate the spruces, but I don't.
They look cheerful, and I like the way,
after a storm, raindrops hang from the tips
of their bristly fingers. Now the cut trees lie
scattered over the hillside, like fallen soldiers.
I begin to gather them up in great armfuls,
as many as I can hold, then carry them awkwardly
into the woods, and throw them down the gully.
I am stumbling with one of these unwieldy bundles,
hugging its prickly green mass to my chest
as if I were in love with it, when I hear

my father thank me. I heave the load
over the edge, and pause to think. Am I
still trying to please him, even in death?
I don't know the answer, and keep going,
thinking, *Would that necessarily be a bad thing?*
and: *This needs to be done, and I'm doing it.*
"You have to do it every year," he told me
last summer, his last one here. I answer now,
"I know. Otherwise they'll take over."
"—take over the world," I hear him echo,
sounding a little paranoid, but I know he's joking.

"The Green Menace," I say. "They've infiltrated
the ecosystem and must be rooted out!"
After a pause, he says, "They breed like rabbits,"
and I point out that now we're mixing metaphors.
And the conversation goes on in my head
as I keep working through the afternoon,
unable to stop myself (the same way he
did chores), sweating, my heart pounding,
struggling with the bundles, hugging them
then heaving them into the gully.

Brenda Hillman

The Mostly Everything That Everyone Is
for BIH

My younger brother, a dutiful brave person, spends his work life
      studying the chestnut fungus *Cryphonectria parasitica* so
      American Chestnut trees will not entirely vanish;

i'm especially glad for his work when i'm trying to get the skins off the
      brain-shaped nuts with their curly, dented integuments.

He was the cheerful child in the family, less seized than his siblings by
      the idea that to please his parents even somewhat we had to be
      almost or completely perfect at each task.

It seems his studied fungus makes cankers of two types: either they swell
      or sink. If sinking cankers, the wound kills the tree; it "knows"
      at its wound level what a life force is. Some genes that hurt the
      fungus help the tree. If the tree dies, the disease has become
      visible or it is visible because it dies.

Most of life's processes are repeatable—at first I wrote "all of life's" but
      that's so not true. Nerve-like structures fall from clouds only
      once. A shorter dawn sets in before the main dawn. Millions
      rise & go faithfully to work, taking their resolve, each person
      clears one throat, music is note by note,

my brother gets our elderly mother up, others in his family rise, he goes
      to his job free of self pity, the suppressed cheer of his childhood
      transferred

to his lab mates who monitor the tiny lives growing without human
      stress, hate, intention or cruelty but also without artful song so
      they dazzle no one.

My brother and i are close as the skin on a chestnut is to the chestnut, as
    close as bark of the tree to its uses. When our mother was sad
    she shut herself in her room, & when she felt better she'd come
    out. You have to slough some things off, she'd say, loving us with
    decades of feral intensity.

He goes along, days pass through the mostly everything that everyone
    is, a sense of continuance is pulled from nothing, something
    produced when it can't stand being nothing, love in the
    experiments, numbers in the mystery, the healing of the
    wound, Psyche sorting seeds like minutes, a wound clinging to
    the tree, sometimes its fruit is food, sometimes the tree is nearly
    perfect waiting

Daniel Lawless

Transmission

to Gellu Naum

...black bloody claws stuck shoulder-high: violence, anguish, absence.
And one must consider also the tree. Imagine
There is an underground mycorrhizal network weaving hyphae
Finer than old men's hair root to root at a cellular level (there is),
A wood-wide web where druggie maples trade tips
On scrounging the best free-sugars, stately sycamores kibbitz, cavil
About the sorry state of bulk pore space, fret about aphids (they do).
Though it's not all scary, or quotidian. A dying birch offers everything
It was so a seedling might get a little sunshine; the neighbors
Chip in, too. How far can we be from the human sensation of grief,
      of joy?
Now about those claw marks. A wound to the one who left them
As to their receptor. The awful news
Announced with a howl; a soughing of limbs, that sudden
Furious murmur of leaves in windless fields.

Lola Haskins

The Discovery

On walking, in my seventies, down a leafy street
behind two women in their early forties who
are chatting to each other as companionably
as birds on a limb, and having thought, with
happy anticipation, ah, I'll be their age soon!
it occurs to me that I've lost my mind—but
just then the clouds evanesce and light pours
through the oaks and ash, to form lace on
the pavement lovely enough to be sewn
into dresses, and I see that time is as
random as the patterns the sun makes on
any given day as it filters through leaves,
and as illusory as a baby being born, and
as strange as the years of our lives that
go by without returning, and as equal as
the one friend's auburn hair and the red leaf
she steps over, which the wind has abandoned
for love of her. And now, having finally
seen that the world is every minute new,
I realize that I'm only a little younger than
those women after all, and I step between
them, and we speak as we walk, and by
the time we part, each of us in her own way
has told the others how lucky she is,
to have been alive in such a beautiful place.

Fred Marchant

Olive Harvest

It's true, the tree has the scent of the sea,
      but the silver leaves, their slender fingers,

the thick, infinitely twined trunk, some riddle
      in the roots that lets it drink from the stones,

even the place where a limb has broken or
      been lopped off, the shoot that springs back

to life, stumps that burn for hour upon hour,
      a scattered discard twig you press to your lips,

and the fruit that hangs from young branches
      and old, a green reddening to black, this fruit

ripened on enough bloodshed and hardened
      human behavior to make you think it will turn

away in disgust, year after suffering year
      comes back, as if to say *here & here & here*

Joyce Wilson

The Etymology of Spruce

> Spruce. Also Sprws, Sprwys,
> Sprewse, Sprewsce, Sprusse,
> Spruse, Sprus, Spruch...
> Pruce, Prussia...Sprutia.
> From *The Oxford English Dictionary*

Spruce: sprout, fermentation, country, tree.

Also *Sprws, Sprwys.* In the ground a single seed, then a tiered cone of consonants and vowels.

Sprewse, Sprewsce. A latticework of branches strewn beneath bright
  skies.

Sprusse. Night winds whisper of rivers and silk.

Spruse, Sprus, Spruch... A house, many houses, cobbled thoroughfares
along an aqueduct,

Pruce, Prussia... hurrying footsteps running through the hard,
  rain-glistened streets—

Sprutia. On the edge of a field, the quiet revelry of a grove of fir trees.

Rosanna Warren

For Chiara

Leaves crackle beneath our feet—tinder, kindling—
as we walk by the brook, the crab-apple tree
a crimson pointilliste nimbus.
You want to hold each wounded soul in your hands.
Autumn flares. The damaged, the human berserk,
find their way to you. I don't know how you sleep.
In the Gorgon's blood, one drop is poison, the other heals.
Fevered autumn, autumn I adore
croons an old song. We stroll the road
scuffing dust. And come upon
a garter snake lying motionless,
its tail, we guess, nicked by a passing car.
When we nudge it, it flips to its back in an agonized S,
squirms, but can't advance. Its belly gleams.
We edge it into the grass. Do we stop seeing
when we walk away? The brook prattles on.
Home's far off. Dusk settles, slowly, among leaves.
That's not mercy, scattering from its hands.

About the Poets

Stephen Ackerman worked as an attorney in the Legal Counsel Division of the New York City Law Department for over 30 years, and retired in 2019. His debut poetry collection, *Late Life*, was selected as the winner of the 2020 Gerald Cable Book Award and will be published by Silverfish Review Press in 2022. His poems have appeared in many publications, including *Boulevard, Mudfish, Ploughshares, Plume, Poetry Daily, Salamander*, and *upstreet*.

Jennifer Barber's new collection is *The Sliding Boat Our Bodies Made* (Word Works, 2022). Her previous collections are *Works on Paper* (Word Works), *Given Away* (Kore Press), and *Rigging the Wind* (Kore Press). She served as editor in chief of the literary journal *Salamander*, based at Suffolk University, from 1992 to 2018. Among her favorite trees are oaks, copper beeches, and Japanese maples.

Rick Barot's most recent book of poems, *The Galleons*, was published by Milkweed Editions in 2020 and was longlisted for the National Book Award. His work has appeared in numerous publications, including *Poetry, The New Republic, Tin House, The Kenyon Review*, and *The New Yorker*. He lives in Tacoma, Washington and directs the Rainier Writing Workshop, the low-residency MFA program in creative writing at Pacific Lutheran University.

Ellen Bass's most recent book is *Indigo* (Copper Canyon, 2020). Among her honors are fellowships from the Guggenheim Foundation and the NEA and three Pushcart prizes. She co-edited the first major anthology of women's poetry, *No More Masks!* and co-authored *The Courage to Heal: A Guide for Women Survivors of Child Sexual Abuse*. A Chancellor of the Academy of American Poets, she teaches in Pacific University's MFA in Writing Program.

Robin Becker published six books in the Pitt Poetry Series, most recently *The Black Bear Inside Me* (2018). She taught at MIT (1977-1994) before moving to Penn State, retiring in 2017 as Liberal Arts Research Professor Emerita. Her poems have appeared in *The American*

Poetry Review, *The New York Times*, *The New Yorker*, and other journals. She has received fellowships from the Bunting Institute at Harvard, the NEA, and the Massachusetts Council on the Arts.

Sheila Black is the author most recently of the chapbook *All the Sleep in the World* (Alabrava Press, 2021). Her fifth collection, *Radium Dream*, was recently published by Salmon Poetry. Poems and essays have appeared in *Poetry*, *Kenyon Review Online*, *The Birmingham Review*, *The New York Times*, and elsewhere. She lives in San Antonio, Texas. She is a co-founder of Zoeglossia, a non-profit to build community for poets with disabilities.

Jaswinder Bolina is author of the full-length poetry collections *The 44th of July* (2019), *Phantom Camera* (2013), and *Carrier Wave* (2007), and of the digital chapbook *The Tallest Building in America* (2014). His debut collection of essays *Of Color* was released by McSweeney's in 2020.

Laure-Anne Bosselaar is the author of *The Hour Between Dog and Wolf*, *Small Gods of Grief* (Isabella Gardner Prize, 2001), and *A New Hunger*, an ALA Notable Book. Her latest book, *These Many Rooms*, came out from Four Way Books. The winner of the 2021 James Dickey Poetry Prize, and the recipient of a Pushcart Prize, she edited five anthologies. She teaches at the Solstice Low Residency MFA Program.

Jericho Brown is the author of *The Tradition* (Copper Canyon 2019), for which he won the Pulitzer Prize. He is the recipient of fellowships from the Guggenheim Foundation, the Radcliffe Institute for Advanced Study at Harvard, and the NEA, and he is winner of the Whiting Award. Brown's first book, *Please* (New Issues, 2008), won the American Book Award. His second, *The New Testament* (Copper Canyon 2014), won the Anisfield-Wolf Book Award.

Stephanie Burt is Professor of English at Harvard. Her most recent books include *After Callimachus* (Princeton, 2020) and *Don't Read Poetry: A Book About How to Read Poems* (Basic, 2019). A new full-length book of her own poems, *We Are Mermaids*, will appear from

Graywolf in 2022. She's @accommodatingly on Twitter, where she has way too much to say about the X-Men.

Victoria Chang's most recent poetry book is *OBIT* (Copper Canyon Press). Her book of hybrid essays, *Dear Memory*, was published by Milkweed Editions in 2021. She lives in Los Angeles and serves as the program chair of Antioch's low-residency MFA program.

Teresa Mei Chuc (birth name: Chúc Mỹ Tuệ), author of three collections of poetry, *Red Thread* (2012), *Keeper of the Winds* (2014), and *Invisible Light* (2018), was born in Sài Gòn, Việt Nam, fled the country as a boat refugee, and immigrated to the U.S. under political asylum shortly after the American war in Việt Nam while her father remained in a Việt Cộng "reeducation" prison camp for nine years. Teresa teaches literature and writing at a public high school in Los Angeles.

Patricia Clark is the author of six books of poetry, most recently *Self-Portrait with a Million Dollars* (Terrapin, 2020), and the author of three chapbooks. New work appears in *Plume, Tar River Poetry, Paterson Literary Review, Westchester Review, I-70 Review, Atticus Review, Midwest Quarterly*, and elsewhere. She is professor emerita of Writing at Grand Valley State University.

Tiana Clark is the author of the poetry collections *I Can't Talk About the Trees Without the Blood* (Univ. of Pittsburgh Press, 2018), winner of the 2017 Agnes Lynch Starrett Prize, and *Equilibrium* (Bull City Press, 2016), selected by Afaa Michael Weaver for the 2016 Frost Place Chapbook Competition. Clark is a winner for the 2020 Kate Tufts Discovery Award and a 2019 NEA Literature Fellow. She is a recipient of the 2021-2022 Amy Lowell Poetry Traveling Scholarship and a 2019 Pushcart Prize.

Eileen Cleary is the author of *Child Ward of the Commonwealth* (Main Street Rag Press, 2019), which received an honorable mention for the Sheila Margaret Motton Book Prize, and *2 a.m. with Keats* (Nixes Mate, 2021). She co-edited the anthology *Voices Amidst the Virus*, which was the featured text at the 2021 MSU Filmetry Festival. Cleary founded and edits the *Lily Poetry Review* and Lily Poetry Review Books, and curates the Lily Poetry Salon.

Anthony Cody is the author of *Borderland Apocrypha* (Omnidawn, 2020), winner of the 2018 Omnidawn Open Book Contest selected by Mei-mei Berssenbrugge. He is a 2021 American Book Award Winner, a 2020 Poets & Writers debut poet, and a 2020 Southwest Book Award Winner. His collection was named a finalist for the National Book Award in Poetry, the PEN America/Jean Stein Book Award, and the LA Times Book Award in Poetry.

Charles Coe is the author of three books of poetry: *All Sins Forgiven: Poems for My Parents*, *Picnic on the Moon*, and *Memento Mori*, all published by Leapfrog Press. He is also the author of *Spin Cycles*, a novella published by Gemma Media. He is adjunct professor of English at Salve Regina University in Newport, Rhode Island, and Bay Path University, where he teaches in their MFA programs.

Andrea Cohen's most recent poetry collection is *Everything*. She directs the Blacksmith House Poetry Series in Cambridge, MA.

Elizabeth J. Coleman is editor of *Here: Poems for the Planet* (Copper Canyon Press, 2019). Author of two poetry collections published by Spuyten Duyvil Press (*Proof* and *The Fifth Generation*) and two poetry chapbooks, she translated the sonnet collection *Pythagore, Amoureux* into French (Folded Word Press, 2016). Her poems appear in a number of journals and anthologies. Having received an MFA from Vermont College of Arts in 2012 after a career as a public interest attorney, she also teaches mindfulness.

Martha Collins's tenth book of poetry, *Because What Else Could I Do* (University of Pittsburgh Press, 2019), won the Poetry Society of America's William Carlos Williams Award. Previous volumes include *Blue Front*, *White Papers*, *Admit One: An American Scrapbook*, and the paired volumes *Day Unto Day* and *Night Unto Night*. Collins founded the U. Mass.-Boston creative writing program, and later taught at Oberlin College. Her eleventh book of poems, *Casualty Reports*, is forthcoming from Pittsburgh in fall 2022. Her website is marthacollinspoet.com.

Robert Cording taught English and creative writing at College of the Holy Cross for thirty-eight years and worked as a poetry mentor in the Seattle Pacific University MFA program. He has published nine collections of poems, the latest of which is *Without My Asking*, and a volume of essays on poetry and religion, *Finding the World's Fullness*. A tenth book of poems and prose meditations, *In the Unwalled City*, is due in 2022.

Kelly Cressio-Moeller is a poet and visual artist. Her poems have been nominated for Pushcart Prizes, Best New Poets, and Best of the Net, appearing widely in journals including *North American Review*, *Salamander*, *Thrush Poetry Journal*, *Water~Stone Review*, and *ZYZZYVA*. She is an associate editor at Glass Lyre Press and lives in the Bay Area. *Shade of Blue Trees* (Two Sylvias Press, Finalist for the Wilder Prize) is her first poetry collection. Visit www.kellycressiomoeller.com.

Yasmine Dalena is from Southern California. She studied at San Diego State University and the University of Virginia. Her work has appeared in *Michigan Quarterly Review* and *Iron Horse Literary Review*.

Toi Derricotte is the recipient of the 2021 Wallace Stevens Award from the Academy of American Poets and the 2020 Frost Medal from the Poetry Society of America. *I: New and Selected Poems* was shortlisted for the National Book Award. She is the co-founder of the Cave Canem Foundation, a home for black poetry.

Lynn Domina is the author of two collections of poetry, *Corporal Works* and *Framed in Silence*, and the editor of a collection of essays, *Poets on the Psalms*. She currently serves as Head of the English Department at Northern Michigan University and as Creative Writing Editor of *The Other Journal*. She lives with her family in Marquette, Michigan, along the beautiful shores of Lake Superior.

Camille T. Dungy is the author of four collections of poetry, most recently *Trophic Cascade*, winner of the Colorado Book Award, and the essay collection *Guidebook to Relative Strangers: Journeys into Race, Motherhood and History*, finalist for the National Book Critics Circle Award. She has edited three anthologies, including *Black Nature: Four Centuries of African American Nature Poetry*. Her honors include the 2021 Academy of American Poets Fellowship, a Guggenheim Fellowship, an American Book Award, and NEA Fellowships in both poetry and prose. She lives in Colorado with her husband and daughter, where she is a University Distinguished Professor at Colorado State University.

Alan Feldman is the author of *The Golden Coin; Immortality; A Sail to Great Island; The Happy Genius*, and other collections. He has completed another, as well as a selection of love poems to be called, *In the First Half-Century that I've Loved You*, with paintings by Nan Hass Feldman. The couple lives in Framingham, Massachusetts.

David Ferry's highly praised translation of *Virgil's Aeneid* was published by the University of Chicago Press in 2017. He is the author of many books of poetry and works of translation, and his poetry collection *Bewilderment* received the 2012 National Book Award for Poetry. Among many other honors, Ferry was awarded the Ruth Lilly Poetry Prize for Lifetime Achievement in 2011.

Jean-Luc Fontaine is a Tucson-based poet. He works full-time as a high school English teacher and part-time as a grocery bagger. In his free time, he likes instant coffee and long hikes to look at strange cactuses.

Jennifer Franklin's most recent collection is *No Small Gift* (Four Way Books, 2018). Her third book, *If Some God Shakes Your House*, will be published by Four Way Books in 2023. Her work has appeared in *The American Poetry Review, Bennington Review, Boston Review, Gettysburg Review, JAMA, The Nation, The Paris Review*, "poem-a-day" on poets. org, *Prairie Schooner*, and *Rhino*. She teaches manuscript revision at the Hudson Valley Writers Center, where she is Program Director. She lives in New York City.

Erica Funkhouser's collections of poetry include *Post & Rail* (2017 winner of The Idaho Prize from Lost Horse Press) and five books published by Houghton Mifflin Harcourt and Alice James Books. Her poems, stories, and essays have appeared in *Agni*, *The Atlantic*, *Harvard Review*, *Massachusetts Review*, *The Nation*, *The New Yorker*, *The Paris Review*, *Poetry*, and other magazines. She lives in Essex, Massachusetts, and teaches poetry-writing at MIT.

Tess Gallagher is an award-winning poet and short-story writer. Her many volumes of poetry include *Midnight Lantern: New and Selected Poems* (2011) and *Is, Is Not* (2019). She has won numerous awards for her work, including fellowships from the Guggenheim Foundation and the NEA, and a Maxine Cushing Gray Foundation Award.

Ross Gay's previous books include *Against Which; Bringing the Shovel Down*; and *Catalog of Unabashed Gratitude*, winner of the 2015 National Book Critics Circle Award and the 2016 Kingsley Tufts Poetry Award. His book *Be Holding: A Poem*, was released in 2020 (Univ. of Pittsburgh Press). His collection of essays, *The Book of Delights*, was released by Algonquin Books in 2019.

Jessica Goodfellow is an American poet living in Japan. Her most recent book *Whiteout* (Univ. of Alaska Press) is about the death of her uncle during an expedition to Denali. Other books are *Mendeleev's Mandala*, *The Insomniac's Weather Report*, and the chapbook *A Pilgrim's Guide to Chaos in the Heartland*. She served as writer-in-residence at Denali National Park and Preserve. Her work has appeared in *Best American Poetry*, *Scientific American*, and *The Southern Review*.

Jessica Greenbaum is a poet, teacher, and social worker. Her most recent volume of poems is *Spilled and Gone* (Univ. of Pittsburgh Press, 2019), and she co-edited the first-ever poetry haggadah, *Mishkan HaSeder: A Passover Haggadah* (CCAR, 2021). A recipient of awards from the NEA and Poetry Society of America, she teaches inside and outside academia, including for communities who may have experienced trauma, and around the relationship of Jewish text to contemporary poems. Visit https://poemsincommunity.org/.

Rachel Eliza Griffiths is a poet, novelist, and visual artist. Her most recent collection of poetry, *Seeing the Body* (W.W. Norton, 2020), was selected as the winner of the 2021 Hurston/Wright Foundation Legacy Award in Poetry, the winner of the 2021 Paterson Poetry Prize, and selected as a finalist for the 2020 NAACP Image Award. Griffiths is the recipient of fellowships from Cave Canem, Kimbilio, and Yaddo. She lives in New York City.

Kelle Groom's poetry collections include *Underwater City* (2004); *Luckily* (2006), which won a Florida Book Award; *Five Kingdoms* (2010), also a Florida Book Award winner; and *Spill* (2017).

Rachel Hadas's latest books *Piece by Piece* (prose) and *Love & Dread* (poetry) were published in the summer of 2021. A new collection of poems, *Pandemic Almanac*, is due out in the spring of 2022. The recipient of numerous awards, Rachel is Board of Governors Professor of English at Rutgers-Newark, where she has taught for many years.

Golan Haji is a Syrian-Kurdish poet, essayist and translator living in France. He has published five books of poems in Arabic: *He Called Out in The Dark* (2004), *Someone Sees You as a Monster* (2008), *Autumn, Here, Is Magical and Vast* (2013), *Scale of Injury* (2016), *Dogs and Beggars* (2022).

Joy Harjo, the 23rd U.S. Poet Laureate and member of the Muscogee Nation, is the author of nine books of poetry, several plays, children's books, two memoirs, and seven music albums. Her honors include the Ruth Lilly Prize from Poetry Foundation, The Academy of American Poets Wallace Stevens Award, two NEA fellowships, a Guggenheim Fellowship, and a Tulsa Artist Fellowship. She is a chancellor of the Academy of American Poets and Chair of the Native Arts & Cultures Foundation.

Jeffrey Harrison is the author of six books of poetry, including, most recently, *Between Lakes* (Four Way Books, 2020) and *Into Daylight* (Tupelo Press, 2014), winner of the Dorset Prize. He has received fellowships from the Guggenheim Foundation and the NEA, among other honors, and his poems have appeared widely in magazines and anthologies, including *The Best American Poetry* and the Pushcart Prize volumes. He lives in Massachusetts and can also be found at jeffreyharrisonpoet.com.

Leslie Harrison's second book, *The Book of Endings* (Akron, 2017), was a finalist for the National Book Award. Her first book, *Displacement* (Mariner, 2009), won the Bakeless Prize in poetry from The Bread Loaf Writers' Conference. A recent recipient of a fellowship from the NEA, she lives in Baltimore and teaches at Towson University.

Lola Haskins' most recent book of poems, *Asylum: Improvisations on John Clare* (Univ. of Pittsburgh Press, 2019) was featured in *The New York Times* Sunday Magazine. Past honors include The Iowa Poetry Prize, two NEAs, two Florida Book Awards, a Florida's Eden prize for environmental writing, and The Writer Magazine / Emily Dickinson Award from Poetry Society of America. She serves as Honorary Chancellor of the Florida State Poets Association.

Robert Hass is most recently the author of *Summer Snow*, a book of poems. He served as Poet Laureate of the United States from 1995 to 1997 and is a professor of English emeritus at the University of California Berkeley.

Robert Hedin is the author, translator, and editor of two dozen books of poetry and prose. The recipient of many honors and awards for his work, he has taught at the University of Alaska, the University of Minnesota, St. Olaf College, and Wake Forest University. He is co-founder and former director of the Anderson Center at Tower View, a residential artist retreat, in Red Wing, Minnesota.

Bob Hicok's poetry volumes include, among others, *Words for Empty, Words for Full* (2010); *Elegy Owed* (2013), a finalist for the National Book Critics Circle Award; and *Sex & Love* (2016). His work has been selected numerous times for *The Best American Poetry* series. Hicok has won Pushcart Prizes and fellowships from the Guggenheim Foundation and the NEA, and has taught creative writing at Western Michigan University and Virginia Tech.

Brenda Hillman is the author of ten collections of poetry from Wesleyan University Press. *In a Few Minutes Before Later* is forthcoming in 2022. A Chancellor Emerita for the Academy of American Poets, she directs the Poetry Week at Community of Writers and teaches at Saint Mary's College of California. For more information see http://blueflowerarts.com/artist/brenda-hillman/.

Edward Hirsch, a MacArthur Fellow, has published ten books of poems, most recently *The Living Fire* (2010), *Gabriel: A Poem* (2014), and *Stranger by Night* (2020). He has also published six prose books about poetry, including *The Essential Poet's Glossary* (2017) and *100 Poems to Break Your Heart* (2021). His new book is *The Heart of American Poetry* (2022). He is president of the John Simon Guggenheim Memorial Foundation and lives in Brooklyn.

Jane Hirshfield's most recent, ninth poetry collection, *Ledger* (Knopf, 2020), centers on the crises of biosphere and social justice. Her work appears in *The New York Times*, *The Guardian*, *TLS*, and ten editions of *The Best American Poetry*. A former chancellor of the Academy of American Poets, in 2019 she was inducted into the American Academy of Arts & Sciences.

Sy Hoahwah (Yapai Nʉʉ/Kwaharʉ/Southern Arapaho) is an enrolled member of the Comanche Nation of Oklahoma. He received his MFA in Creative Writing from the University of Arkansas. Hoahwah is the author of three collections of poetry, *Ancestral Demon of a Grieving Bride* (Univ. of New Mexico Press, 2021), *Night Cradle* (USPOCO Books, 2011), and *Velroy and the Madischie Mafia* (West End Press, 2009). In 2013, Sy was a recipient of the NEA Literature Fellowship. He resides with his wife and daughter outside of Little Rock, Arkansas.

Ishion Hutchinson was born in Port Antonio, Jamaica. He is the author of the poetry collections *Far District* and *House of Lords and Commons*. He directs the Graduate Creative Writing Program at Cornell University.

Major Jackson is the author of five books of poetry, including *The Absurd Man* (2020), *Roll Deep* (2015), *Holding Company* (2010), *Hoops* (2006), and *Leaving Saturn* (2002), which won the Cave Canem Poetry Prize for a first book of poems. He is a recipient of fellowships from the Fine Arts Work Center in Provincetown, Guggenheim Foundation, NEA, and Radcliffe Institute for Advanced Study at Harvard University.

Maya Janson's second poetry collection, *On the Mercy Me Planet*, will be published by Blue Edge Books in 2022. Her poems have appeared in *The New Yorker*, *The Best American Poetry*, and elsewhere. She lives with her family in western Massachusetts.

Richard Jones has published more than a dozen poetry collections, including *Stranger on Earth* (2018), *The King of Hearts* (2016), *The Correct Spelling & Exact Meaning* (2009), *Apropos of Nothing* (2006), and *The Blessing: New and Selected Poems* (2000), which won The Midland Authors Award.

Fady Joudah has published five poetry collections, *Textu* and *Tethered to Stars* among them.

George Kalogeris's most recent book of poems is *Winthropos* (Louisiana State Univ. Press, 2021). He is also the author of *Guide to Greece* (LSU); a book of paired poems in translation, *Dialogos* (Antilever); and poems based on the notebooks of Albert Camus, *Camus: Carnets* (Pressed Wafer). His poems and translations have been anthologized in *Joining Music with Reason*, chosen by Christopher Ricks (Waywiser).

Judy Katz's poems have appeared on *Poetry Daily* and in *The New York Times Book Review*, *Salamander*, *The Women's Review of Books*, *Plume*, *upstreet*, and other print and online journals. Her work has been nominated for a Pushcart Prize and widely anthologized. Judy is a native of Memphis, Tennessee, where she grew up on both Tall Trees Drive and Shady Grove Road. She was clearly meant to live among trees.

Ellen Kaufman runs daily through the majestic trees of Riverside Park, in upper Manhattan. She is the author of *House Music* (2013) and *Double-Parked, with Tosca* (2021), both from Able Muse Press. Her poems have appeared in *Epoch*, *Southwest Review*, *The New Yorker*, *The Yale Review*, and elsewhere. After many years reviewing poetry for *Library Journal*, she now reviews for *Publishers Weekly*. The poem included here celebrates a famous cherry grove in suburban Maryland.

John Koethe is the author of several collections of poetry, including *North Point North: New and Selected* (2002), *Ninety-fifth Street* (2009), *ROTC Kills* (2012), *The Swimmer* (2016), and *Walking Backwards: Poems 1966-2016* (2018). He teaches philosophy, focusing on the philosophy of language.

Yusef Komunyakaa's numerous books of poetry include *Dien Cai Dau*, *Neon Vernacular*, for which he received the Pulitzer Prize, *Warhorses*, *Emperor of Water Clocks*, and most recently *Everyday Mojo Songs of Earth: New and Selected Poems, 2001-2021*. His honors include the William Faulkner Prize (Université Rennes, France), the Ruth Lilly Poetry Prize, the Wallace Stevens Award, the 2021 Griffin Lifetime Recognition Award, and the 2021 Zbigniew Herbert International Literary Award.

Ted Kooser's most recent collection of poems is *Red Stilts*, from Copper Canyon Press. He has a chapbook forthcoming from Pulley Press, a children's picture book from Candlewick Press, and a collection of poems for young people from University of Nebraska Press, all due out in 2022.

Lance Larsen has published five poetry collections, most recently *What the Body Knows* (Tampa, 2018). His awards include a Pushcart Prize, The Tampa Review Prize, The Sewanee Review Prize, and an NEA fellowship. He teaches at BYU and fools around with aphorisms: "When climbing a new mountain, wear old shoes." In 2017, he completed a five-year appointment as Poet Laureate of Utah. He likes to run the Bonneville Shoreline Trail near his house and sometimes he juggles.

Daniel Lawless's book, *The Gun My Sister Killed Herself With*, was published in 2018. He has recent/forthcoming poems in *Field, Barrow Street, Prairie Schooner, Ploughshares, Poetry International, Los Angeles Review, upstreet, Massachusetts Review*, and *Dreaming Awake: New Prose Poetry from the U.S., Australia, and the U.K.* A recipient of a continuing Shifting Foundation grant, he is the founder and editor of *Plume: A Journal of Contemporary Poetry*, Plume Editions, and the annual *Plume Poetry* anthologies.

Deborah Leipziger is a poet, author, and advisor on sustainability. Her chapbook, *Flower Map*, was published by Finishing Line Press (2013). Born in Brazil, she is the author of several books on sustainability. Nominated three times for a Pushcart Prize, her poems have been published in *Salamander, Lily Poetry Review*, and *POESY*, among other places. Her collection of poems *Story & Bone* is forthcoming from Lily Poetry Review Books in January 2023.

Debora Lidov is the author of the chapbook *Trance* (Finishing Line Press, 2015). Her poems have appeared in numerous journals, including *The Paris Review, Salamander, upstreet*, and *Tarpaulin Sky*. She is a medical social worker and lives in Brooklyn.

Carol Light received the Robert H. Winner award from the Poetry Society of America in 2013 and an award from Artist Trust in 2012. Her poems have appeared in *Poetry Northwest, Narrative Magazine, American Life in Poetry, 32 Poems*, and elsewhere. Her collection *Heaven from Steam* was a finalist for the 2012 Able Muse Book Award.

Ada Limón is the author of six books of poetry, including *The Carrying*, which won the National Book Critics Circle Award for Poetry. Limón is also the host of the critically acclaimed poetry podcast, *The Slowdown*.

Esther Lin was born in Rio de Janeiro, Brazil, and lived in the United States as an undocumented immigrant for 21 years. She is the author of *The Ghost Wife*, winner of the 2017 Poetry Society of America Chapbook Fellowship. In 2020 she was a Writing Fellow at the Fine Arts Work Center, and from 2017 to 2019, a Wallace Stegner Fellow.

Currently she is a writing fellow at Cité internationale, Paris, and co-organizes the Undocupoets, a group that raises consciousness about the structural barriers undocumented poets face.

Maurice Manning has published seven books of poetry. He lives with his family in Kentucky.

Fred Marchant is the author of five books of poetry, the most recent of which, *Said Not Said*, was published by Graywolf Press in 2017. Graywolf also published his collections *Full Moon Boat* (2000) and *The Looking House* (2009). His first book, *Tipping Point*, won the 1993 Washington Prize from the Word Works. In 2002 Dedalus Press of Dublin, Ireland, brought out his collection *House on Water, House in Air*.

Peter Marcus's collection *Dark Square* was published by Pleasure Boat Studio in 2012. His poems have appeared widely in literary journals, as well as in two human rights anthologies: *Before We Have Nowhere To Stand: Poems on Israel and Palestine*, and *I Go To Ruined Places: Contemporary Poems in Defense of Global Human Rights*, both published by Lost Horse Press.

Jennifer Markell's first poetry collection, *Samsara* (Turning Point, 2014) was named a "Must Read" book by The Massachusetts Book Awards. Her second collection, *Singing at High Altitude*, was published by The Main Street Rag in 2021. Jennifer's work has appeared in *Bitter Oleander*, *Cimarron Review*, *Consequence*, and *Rhino*, among other publications. She works as a psychotherapist, serves on the board of the New England Poetry Club, and tends two gardens and three well-versed cats.

Gretchen Marquette is the author of *May Day* (Graywolf Press, 2016.) Her poetry has appeared in *Poetry*, *Harper's*, *The Paris Review*, *Tin House*, and elsewhere. She lives in Minneapolis.

Khaled Mattawa, born and raised in Benghazi, Libya, came to the United States as a teenager. His several collections of poetry include

Fugitive Atlas (2020), *Tocqueville* (2010), *Amorisco* (2008), *Zodiac of Echoes* (2003), and *Ismailia Eclipse* (1995). He has translated numerous volumes of contemporary Arabic poetry.

Gail Mazur's recent poetry collections include *Land's End: New and Selected Poems* (2020), *Forbidden City* (2016), and *Figures in a Landscape* (2011). She has taught widely and is the recipient of numerous grants and awards. She is the founder of the Blacksmith House Poetry Series, one of the oldest ongoing reading series in the country.

Frances McCue is a poet and prose writer from Seattle. Her books include *The Bled, I Almost Read the Books Whole, Timber Curtain*, and *The Car That Brought You Here Still Runs: Revisiting the Northwest Towns of Richard Hugo*. She is the founding editor of Pulley Press, a new poetry publishing imprint that celebrates poetry from the rural Americas.

Lynne McMahon has published four collections of poetry, including *Sentimental Standards*. The recipient of an Award for Literary Excellence from the American Academy of Arts and Letters, she has also been awarded grants from the Guggenheim Foundation, the Ingram Merrill Foundation, and the Missouri Arts Council.

Diane Mehta is the author of the poetry collection *Forest with Castanets*. She received a 2020 Spring Literature grant from the Café Royal Cultural Foundation for her nonfiction writing. Recent poems and essays are in *The New Yorker, The American Poetry Review, Agni*, and *Harvard Divinity Bulletin*. She was a 2021 fellow at Civitella Ranieri in Italy. She lives in Brooklyn.

Philip Metres has written numerous books, including *Shrapnel Maps* (Copper Canyon, 2020). Winner of Guggenheim, Lannan, and NEA fellowships, he is professor of English and director of the Peace, Justice, and Human Rights program at John Carroll University, and core faculty at Vermont College of Fine Arts MFA. He believes that trees know more than they are saying.

Kamilah Aisha Moon was an American poet who published two books of poetry: *She Has a Name* and *Starshine & Clay*, both from Four Way Books. She was a beloved member of the faculty at Agnes Scott College. She passed away in the fall of 2021.

Mihaela Moscaliuc is the author of the poetry collections *Cemetery Ink, Immigrant Model*, and *Father Dirt*, translator of Liliana Ursu's *Clay and Star* and Carmelia Leonte's *The Hiss of the Viper*, editor of *Insane Devotion: On the Writing of Gerald Stern*, and co-editor of *Border Lines: Poems of Migration*. She is the translation editor for *Plume* and associate professor of English at Monmouth University, New Jersey.

D. Nurkse is the author of twelve poetry collections, including the new and selected volume *A Country of Strangers* (Knopf, 2022).

Naomi Shihab Nye is the Young People's Poet Laureate (Poetry Foundation). Palestinian-American, she has been a visiting writer in hundreds of schools and communities all over the world for many years. *19 Varieties of Gazelle: Poems of the Middle East*, was a finalist for the National Book Award. *The Turtle of Oman* (Greenwillow, 2014) will be followed by *The Turtle of Michigan* in 2022. Her book *The Tiny Journalist* won both Texas poetry awards (Texas Institute of Letters and Writers League) in 2020.

Ed Ochester's collections of poetry include *Sugar Run Road* (2015); *The Land of Cockaigne* (2001); and *Unreconstructed: Poems Selected and New* (2007), among others. He founded the literary journal *5AM* and served as a longtime editor of the Pitt Poetry Series at the University of Pittsburgh Press.

Rebecca Okrent's father invited her into the world of poetry by suggesting she write rather than brood about a sister's slight. The result was a poem about perspective that used a tree as metaphor. She was seven when she made her covenant with nature and the reading and writing of poetry. Being a nun was briefly in play. Her collection *Boys of My Youth* was published in 2015 by Four Way Books.

Sharon Olds has written twelve books of poetry. *Balladz* will come out from Knopf in September 2022. *Arias* (2019) was short-listed for the 2020 Griffin Poetry Prize, and *Stag's Leap* (2012) received the Pulitzer Prize and England's T. S. Eliot Prize. Olds is the Erich Maria Remarque Professor of Creative Writing in New York University's Graduate Creative Writing Program. She lives in New York City.

William Olsen's most recent book of poetry is *TechnoRage* (Northwestern). His work has been awarded fellowships from the NEA, the Guggenheim Foundation, and Breadloaf. He lives in Kalamazoo.

Alicia Suskin Ostriker has published 19 collections of poetry, been twice nominated for the National Book Award, and has twice received the National Jewish Book Award for Poetry, among other honors. Her most recent collections of poems are *Waiting for the Light* and *The Volcano and After: Selected and New Poems* 2002-2019. She was New York State Poet Laureate for 2018-2021 and a Chancellor of the Academy of American Poets in 2015-2020.

Cecily Parks is the author of two poetry collections and editor of the anthology *The Echoing Green: Poems of Fields, Meadows, and Grasses* (2016). Her poems appear in *The New Yorker, The Best American Poetry 2020, The Best American Poetry 2021*, and elsewhere. The poetry editor for *ISLE: Interdisciplinary Studies in Literature and Environment*, she teaches in the MFA Program in Creative Writing at Texas State University.

Linda Pastan's 14th book of poems, *Insomnia*, was published in 2015 and won the Towson University Prize for Literature. She has twice been a finalist for the National Book Award, and in 2003 she won the Ruth Lilly Prize for Lifetime Achievement. *A Dog Runs Through It* was published in 2018 and *Almost An Elegy* is due in 2022. She is a past Poet Laureate of Maryland.

Marsha Pomerantz's writing often turns toward the visual, and she is now experimenting with dialogue between photos and text. Claire Illouz (claire-illouz.com) made an artist's book from her poem "They

Run," with engravings and etchings (2016). Publications include *The Illustrated Edge* (Biblioasis, 2011) and poems and essays in/at *Beloit Poetry Journal*, berfrois.com, *Best American Essays 2016*, *Boston Review*, broadsidedpress.org, *Harvard Review, Parnassus, PN Review*, poetrynet.org, quidditylit.org, *Raritan*, and *Salamander*. More at marshapomerantz.org.

Jacquelyn Pope is a poet and translator whose work has been published in *The New Yorker, Poetry, The New Republic*, and elsewhere. Her books include *Watermark, Dreamboat*, and a selection of poems by the Dutch poet Hester Knibbe, *Hungerpots*.

Khadijah Queen, PhD, is the author of six books, including *I'm So Fine: A List of Famous Men & What I Had On* (2017), praised in *O Magazine, The New Yorker, Rain Taxi, Los Angeles Review*, and elsewhere. An essay about the pandemic, "False Dawn," appears in *Harper's Magazine*. Her latest book, *Anodyne* (Tin House 2020), is the winner of the William Carlos Williams Book Award for poetry. She is an associate professor of creative writing at Virginia Tech.

Donald Revell is the author of sixteen collections of poetry, most recently of *White Campion* (2021) and *The English Boat* (2018), both from Alice James Books. Revell has also published six volumes of translations from the French, including Apollinaire's *Alcools*, Rimbaud's *A Season in Hell*, Laforgue's *Last Verses*, and Verlaine's *Songs without Words*. Winner of the PEN USA Translation Award and two-time winner of the PEN USA Award for Poetry, he has also won the Academy of American Poets' Lenore Marshall Prize and is a former fellow of the Ingram Merrill and Guggenheim Foundations.

James Richardson (www.aboutjamesrichardson.com) keeps *The American Heritage Dictionary of Indo-European Roots* on his desk at all times. His most recent collection of poems and aphorisms is *For Now* (Copper Canyon Press, 2020).

Frances Richey is the author of three poetry collections: *The Warrior* (Viking Penguin 2008), *The Burning Point* (White Pine Press 2004), and the chapbook *Voices of the Guard*, a collaboration with the Oregon National Guard and Clackamas Community College, published by the college in 2010. She teaches an ongoing poetry class at Himan Brown Senior Program at the 92nd Street Y, and is the poetry editor for *upstreet literary magazine*.

Valencia Robin is a poet, painter, and recipient of the NEA Fellowship. Her first collection of poems, *Ridiculous Light*, won Persea Books' Lexi Rudnitsky First Book Prize, was a finalist for the Kate Tufts Discovery Award, and was named one of *Library Journal's* Best Poetry Books of 2019. A Cave Canem fellow, she holds an MFA in Creative Writing from the University of Virginia and an MFA in Art & Design from the University of Michigan.

Kay Ryan was appointed the Library of Congress's sixteenth Poet Laureate Consultant in Poetry in 2008. Her poems have appeared in *The New Yorker*, *The Paris Review*, *The Atlantic Monthly*, *The New Republic*, and other periodicals. She is the recipient of numerous accolades and awards, including the Ruth Lilly Poetry Prize and a Guggenheim Fellowship.

Mary Jo Salter is the author of nine books of poetry published by Knopf, including *Zoom Rooms* (2022). Her book *Nothing by Design* was recipient of the 2015 Poets' Prize. She is a co-editor of *The Norton Anthology of Poetry*, and a lyricist whose work has been performed by Fred Hersch and Renée Fleming. Salter is Krieger-Eisenhower Professor in The Writing Seminars at Johns Hopkins University, and lives in Baltimore.

Cheryl Savageau is the author of the memoir, *Out of the Crazywoods*, and three books of poetry, *Mother/Land*, *Dirt Road Home*, and *Home Country*; and a children's book, *Muskrat Will Be Swimming*. She has won fellowships in poetry from the NEA and the Massachusetts Artists Fellowship Program, and is a three-time fellow at MacDowell. She is the former editor of *Dawnland Voices 2.0*. She teaches Indigenous literatures and creative writing at the Bread Loaf School of English at Middlebury College.

Maxine Scates's fourth collection of poetry is *My Wilderness* (Pitt Poetry Series, 2021). Her poems have been widely published throughout the country in such journals as *Agni, The American Poetry Review, Cave Wall, Copper Nickel, Court Green, New England Review, The New Yorker, Ploughshares, Plume, Poetry,* and *Virginia Quarterly Review,* and have received, among other awards, the Agnes Lynch Starrett Poetry Prize, the Oregon Book Award for Poetry, and two Pushcart Prizes.

Grace Schulman's latest book of poems is *The Marble Bed,* and her recent memoir is *Strange Paradise: Portrait of a Marriage.* She is a member of the American Academy of Arts and Letters, and has been awarded the Frost Medal for Distinguished Lifetime Achievement in American Poetry, given by the Poetry Society of America. Editor of *The Poems of Marianne Moore,* she is Distinguished Professor of English at Baruch College, C.U.N.Y.

Howard Schwartz is Professor Emeritus at the University of Missouri-St. Louis. He has published five books of poetry: *Vessels, Gathering the Sparks, Sleepwalking Beneath the Stars, Breathing in the Dark,* and *The Library of Dreams: New and Selected Poems.* He has also edited a four-volume set of Jewish folktales, which includes *Elijah's Violin & Other Jewish Fairy Tales, Miriam's Tambourine: Jewish Folktales from Around the World, Lilith's Cave: Jewish Tales of the Supernatural,* and *Gabriel's Palace: Jewish Mystical Tales.* He is also the author of *Tree of Souls: The Mythology of Judaism.*

Vijay Seshadri is the author of five collections of poems: *Wild Kingdom, The Long Meadow, The Disappearances, 3 Sections,* and *That Was Now, This Is Then;* and many essays, reviews, and memoir fragments. His work has been recognized with a number of honors, including the Pulitzer Prize for poetry. He teaches at Sarah Lawrence College.

Diane Seuss's most recent collection is *frank: sonnets* (Graywolf Press, 2021). *Still Life with Two Dead Peacocks and a Girl* (Graywolf Press, 2018), was a finalist for the National Book Critics Circle Award and the Los Angeles Times Book Prize in Poetry. *Four-Legged Girl* (Graywolf Press, 2015) was a finalist for the Pulitzer Prize. She was raised by a single mother in rural Michigan, which she continues to call home.

Elaine Sexton is a poet, critic, bookmaker, and educator. Her most recent collection of poetry is *Drive*, published by Grid Books (2022). She lives in New York.

Don Share's books include the poetry collections *Union*, *Squandermania*, and *Wishbone*, and a translation of the selected poems of Miguel Hernández. He is the editor of *Bunting's Persia* and *The Poems of Basil Bunting*.

Evie Shockley's most recent poetry collections, *the new black* (Wesleyan, 2011) and *semiautomatic* (Wesleyan, 2017), both won the Hurston/Wright Legacy Award; the latter was also a finalist for the Pulitzer Prize and the *LA Times* Book Prize. Her poetry has appeared internationally in print and audio formats, in English and in translation. She has received the Lannan Literary Award for Poetry, the Stephen Henderson Award, and the Holmes National Poetry Prize, among other honors. Shockley is Professor of English at Rutgers University.

John Shoptaw, raised among bald cypresses in the Missouri bootheel, lives now among redwoods in the Bay Area, where he teaches at the University of California, Berkeley. His *Times Beach* won the Northern California Book Award in Poetry. He is currently finishing a poetry collection called *Near-Earth Object*.

Tracy K. Smith is the author of *Wade in the Water*, winner of the Anisfield-Wolf Book Award; *Life on Mars*, winner of the Pulitzer Prize; *Duende*, winner of the James Laughlin Award; and *The Body's Question*, winner of the Cave Canem Poetry Prize. She is also the author of a memoir, *Ordinary Light*, which was a finalist for the National Book Award. From 2017 to 2019, Smith served as Poet Laureate of the United States. She teaches at Harvard University.

Kim Stafford is the founding director of the Northwest Writing Institute at Lewis & Clark College, and author of a dozen books of poetry and prose, most recently *Singer Come from Afar* (Red Hen Press, 2021). He served as Oregon Poet Laureate 2018-2020, and has taught writing in Mexico, Scotland, Italy, and Bhutan.

Peter Streckfus is the author of *Errings*, winner of Fordham University Press's 2013 POL Editor's Prize, and *The Cuckoo*, which won the Yale Series of Younger Poets competition in 2003. His awards include fellowships and grants from the Bread Loaf Writers' Conference, the Peter S. Reed Foundation, the American Academy of Arts and Letters, and the American Academy in Rome. He is on the faculty of the Creative Writing Program at George Mason University and is an editorial co-director of *Poetry Daily*.

Jennifer K. Sweeney is the author of four books of poetry, most recently *Foxlogic, Fireweed*, winner of the Backwaters Prize from Backwaters Press/University of Nebraska. Her other collections are *Little Spells*, *How to Live on Bread and Music*, and *Salt Memory*. She is the recipient of many awards, including the James Laughlin Award and a Pushcart Prize. She teaches poetry workshops privately and at the University of Redlands in California.

Arthur Sze's latest book of poetry is *The Glass Constellation: New and Collected Poems* (Copper Canyon Press, 2021). His previous books include *Sight Lines*, which won the 2019 National Book Award for Poetry, *Compass Rose, The Ginkgo Light*, and *Quipu*. He has received many awards, including the 2021 Shelley Memorial Award from the Poetry Society of America. A professor emeritus at the Institute of American Indian Arts, he lives in Santa Fe.

Barbara Thomas is a poet, teacher, and nature writer. Her poems have appeared in *Paterson Literary Review, Fiele-Festa, Lalitamba, Writing Nature*, and others. She is the author of *Seduced by Sighs of Trees* (2007) and *The Last Green Valley* (2019). She lives in Thompson, Connecticut and Cambridge, Massachusetts.

Daniel Tobin is the author of nine books of poems, including *Blood Labors*, named one of the Best Poetry Books of the Year by *The New York Times*. His poetry has won many awards, among them the Julia Ward Howe Award, and fellowships from the NEA and the Guggenheim Foundation. His most recent work is *On Serious Earth: Poetry and Transcendence*. A trilogy of book-length poems, *The Mansions*, will appear in 2023.

Angela Narciso Torres is the author of *What Happens Is Neither* (Four Way Books), *To the Bone* (Sundress Publications), and *Blood Orange* (Willow Books). Recent work appears or is forthcoming in *Poetry*, *Poetry Northwest*, and *Prairie Schooner*. Born in Brooklyn and raised in Manila, she currently resides in San Diego. She serves as a senior and reviews editor for *Rhino Poetry*.

Natasha Trethewey is a former U.S. Poet Laureate and the author of five collections of poetry. Her *New York Times*-bestselling memoir, *Memorial Drive*, was a finalist for the Carnegie Prize and won the 2021 Anisfield-Wolf Book Award for Nonfiction. She is currently the Board of Trustees Professor of English at Northwestern University. In 2007 she won the Pulitzer Prize in Poetry for her collection *Native Guard*.

Brian Turner is the author of a memoir, *My Life as a Foreign Country*, and two collections of poetry, *Here, Bullet* and *Phantom Noise*. He edited *The Kiss* and co-edited *The Strangest of Theatres*. He has published work in *The New York Times*, *National Geographic*, *Harper's*, and other fine journals. He is from California, with its redwoods and giant sequoia trees, though he now lives in Orlando with his dog, Dene, among cypress draped in Spanish moss.

Emily Tuszynska lives beside a hundred-acre patch of successional tuliptree-oak forest growing on former farmland now owned by George Mason University in the suburbs of Washington, D.C. Her poems can be found in many journals, recently including *Mom Egg Review*, *New Ohio Review*, *Prairie Schooner*, and *Southern Poetry Review*.

Connie Wanek is the author of several books of poetry, most recently *Consider the Lilies: Mrs. God Poems*. Forthcoming from Candlewick Press is a book of poems for younger readers that she co-authored with former U.S. Poet Laureate Ted Kooser. She lives near her grandchildren in Minnesota.

Rosanna Warren is the author of six books of poetry, most recently *So Forth* (2020) and *Ghost in a Red Hat* (2011). Her biography of Max Jacob, *Max Jacob: A Life in Art and Letters*, appeared in 2020. She has received awards from the Academy of American Poets, the American Academy of Arts & Letters, the Lila Wallace Foundation, and the Guggenheim Foundation, among others. She teaches at the University of Chicago.

Afaa Michael Weaver's most recent book of poems is *Spirit Boxing*. In spring 2023, Red Hen Press will release his 16th collection, *A Fire in the Hills*. His several plays include *Berea*. Weaver is a Cave Canem Elder.

Gary Whited is a poet, philosopher, and psychotherapist. His book *Having Listened* was the 2013 Homebound Publications Poetry Contest winner. The poems in *Having Listened* speak from the confluence of a childhood on the prairie and an encounter with the voice of Parmenides from ancient Greece. His poems have appeared in journals that include *Salamander*, *Plainsongs*, *The Aurorean*, *Atlanta Review*, and *Comstock Review*.

Leslie Williams is the author of *Even the Dark*, winner of the Crab Orchard Series in Poetry Open Competition, and *Success of the Seed Plants*, winner of the Bellday Prize. Her poems have appeared in *Poetry*, *Kenyon Review*, *Southern Review*, *Image*, *America*, and many other magazines. She lives near Boston.

Joyce Wilson has taught English at Suffolk University and Boston University. She is creator and editor of the *Poetry Porch* (www. poetryporch.com), a literary magazine on the Internet since 1997. Her poems have appeared in many literary journals, among them *Free Inquiry*, *Salamander*, *The Lyric*, and *Poetry Ireland*. Her chapbook *The Need for a Bridge* and her full-length collection *Take and Receive* were both published in 2019.

C. Dale Young is the author of a novel, *The Affliction* (2018), and five collections of poetry, including *Prometeo* (2021) and *The Halo* (2016). A recipient of fellowships from the NEA, the John Simon Guggenheim Memorial Foundation, and the Rockefeller Foundation, Young practices medicine full-time and teaches in the Warren Wilson College MFA Program for Writers. He lives in San Francisco.

Javier Zamora, born in El Salvador, migrated to the United States when he was nine. His first poetry collection, *Unaccompanied*, was published by Copper Canyon in 2017. In his forthcoming memoir, *Solito* (Hogarth, September 2022), he retells his nine-week odyssey across Guatemala, Mexico, and eventually through the Sonoran Desert. Zamora was a 2018-2019 Radcliffe Fellow at Harvard University.

Geraldine Zetzel's poetry collection *Mapping the Sands* was published by Mayapple Press in 2010. Her poetry collection *Traveling Light* was published by Antrim House Books in 2016. She lives in the Boston area.

Linda Stern Zisquit has published five full-length collections of poetry, most recently *Return from Elsewhere* and *Havoc: New & Selected Poems*. Her translations from Hebrew poetry include *Wild Light: Selected Poems of Yona Wallach* and *These Mountains: Selected Poems of Rivka Miriam*. Born in Buffalo, NY, she has lived in Israel since 1978. For many years she was Poetry Coordinator for the Creative Writing Program at Bar Ilan University. She founded and runs Artspace Gallery in Jerusalem.

Permissions

Index of Authors and Titles

32 Views from the Hammock   49
74,000 Acres of Forest Burning   31
Ackerman, Stephen   176
Alleluia   162
Ant Tree   90
Ari in the Forest   166
Artifacts on a Hanging Tree, Goliad, Texas   92
At the Cemetery   158
Autobiographia Literaria   104
Balance, onslaught   39
Barber, Jennifer   95
"Birds small enough"   40
Barot, Rick   116
Bass, Ellen   31
Becker, Robin   139
Black, Sheila   148
Bolina, Jaswinder   33
Bosselaar, Laure-Anne   41
Brown, Jericho   147
Burial   24
Burnished Days   131
Burt, Stephanie   153
Callimachus, Iamb 4, frag. 194   153
Cathedral   180
Cedar Theater   170
Chang, Victoria   38
Cherry Blossoms   106
Choices   20
Chuc, Teresa Mei   46
Clark, Patricia   161
Clark, Tiana   28
Cleary, Eileen   23
Coat   36
Cody, Anthony   92
Coconuts   73

Coe, Charles   63, 151

Cohen, Andrea   27

Coleman, Elizabeth J.   79

Collins, Martha   167

Confessions of a nature lover   45

Conscious Sedation   54

Copper Beech   96

Cording, Robert   158

Corona (1)   148

Cressio-Moeller, Kelly   54

Cri de Coeur   125

Dalena, Yasmine   37

Derricotte, Toi   106

Dogwood Time   101

Domina, Lynn   162

Downdraft   141

Dungy, Camille T.   21

Elegy beginning in the shade of Aunt Mary's mulberry tree   21

Elegy on My Drive Home in the Rain   41

Eulogy   165

Fall   132

Feldman, Alan   137

Ferry, David   127

Find the Hidden Tree   69

First Thought, Best Thought   27

Floodplain   122

Fontaine, Jean-Luc   35

For Chiara   193

Forest and Trees   110

Franklin, Jennifer   129

from Blue Front   167

from Eternity: Landscape Painting   57

from I am a Miner. The Light Burns Blue   38

from Pome: Malus domestica   182

From this bench I like to call my bench I sit   91

Funkhouser, Erica   182

Gallagher, Tess   20

Gay, Ross   24

Gone   102

Goodfellow, Jessica   177

Green Figs   61

Greenbaum, Jessica   77

Grief in Fenceposts   30

Griffiths, Rachel Eliza   128

Groom, Kelle   36

Hadas, Rachel   110

Haji, Golan   64

Harjo, Joy   184

Harrison, Jeffrey   185

Harrison, Leslie   159

Haskins, Lola   190

Hass, Robert   25

He Takes Me to See the Oldest Tree   71

Heave   37

Hedin, Robert   130

Hicok, Bob   45

Hickory Nuts   53

Hillman, Brenda   187

Hirsch, Edward   61

Hirshfield, Jane   68

Hoahwah, Sy   62

How to uproot a tree   78

Humans Naming Trees   177

Hutchinson, Ishion   108

Immortal Stories   50

In a Cemetery under a Walnut Tree That Crows   64

In Lieu of Flowers   109

In November   137

In the Bronx   52

In the Forest of Splintered Trees   35

In the Second Half of Life   124

Inaugural Ball   33

It Begins with the Trees   156

Jackson, Major   134

Janson, Maya   66
Jones, Richard   113
Joudah, Fady   64
Kalogeris, George   111
Katz, Judy   47
Kaufman, Ellen   99
Koethe, John   131
Komunyakaa, Yusef   67
Kooser, Ted   112
Larsen, Lance   49
Lawless, Daniel   189
Leaf Litter   133
Leaves   136
Leipziger, Deborah   178
Lessons from a Tree   169
Lidov, Debora   69
Light, Carol   141
Limen   94
Limón, Ada   156
Lin, Esther   142
Lobo   178
Locust Trees in Late May   112
Lord of Childhood   48
Manning, Maurice   115
Marchant, Fred   191
Marcus, Peter   101
Markell, Jennifer   133
Marquette, Gretchen   163
Mattawa, Khaled   149
Mazur, Gail   81
McCue, Frances   170
McMahon, Lynne   71
Mehta, Diane   50
Memento Mori: Apple Orchard   129
Metres, Philip   72
Mistaking Silence for Consent   79
Model of a Tree Growing in the Path of a Spiral   76

Monarchs, Viceroys, Swallowtails   130
Moon, K.A.   87
More desirable than gold [Psalm 19]   181
Moscaliuc, Mihaela   73
Motion Harmony #2   95
Moved by the Beauty of the Trees   108
Mulberries   151
Mulberries in the Park   114
My City   149
My Father and the Fig Tree   88
New England Camping Ode   172
Not Pigment, Not Truth   175
Nurske, D.   48
Nye, Naomi Shihab   88
Ochester, Ed   132
October   127
October; November   135
Okrent, Rebecca   109
Olds, Sharon   75, 172
Olive Harvest   191
Olsen, William   55
One Tree   72
Ostriker, Alicia Suskin   135
Parable   159
Parks, Cecily   43
Pastan, Linda   150
Peach Tree   86
Pine Tree Ode   75
Pines   83
Pomerantz, Marsha   175
Pope, Jacquelyn   168
Queen, Khadijah   39
Rainforest   46
Ramón   85
Revell, Donald   40
Richardson, James   83
Richey, Frances   85

Robin, Valencia   180

Rudy's Tree   81

Ryan, Kay   65

Saguaros   58

Salter, Mary Jo   100

Savageau, Cheryl   90, 118

Scates, Maxine   119

Schulman, Grace   102

Schwartz, Howard   166

Seshadri, Vijay   74

Seuss, Diane   91

Sexton, Elaine   104

Shady Grove   121

Share, Don   121

Shockley, Evie   19

Shoptaw, John   84

Shore Cedars   55

Smith, Tracy K.   57

So Different   65

Speaking Tree   184

Stafford, Kim   169

Storm-Struck Tree   77

Streckfus, Peter   76

Sweeney, Jennifer K.   78

Sze, Arthur   52, 174

Taking Down the Tree   63

The Ayes Have It   28

The Canopy   161

The Cherries of Kenwood   99

The Discovery   190

The Etymology of Spruce   192

The Grief of Trees   139

The Indiana Bats   43

The Marrow   116

The Mostly Everything That Everyone Is   187

The Oak Tree's Burden   87

The Orchards   119

The Place des Vosges   113
The Problem of Describing Trees   126
The Radiant's   174
The Switch   115
The Tree   80
The Trees   147
The Tree in the Midst   84
The Way We Fled   23
The Willow at Flint Pond   118
The World's Oldest Cherry Tree Is Alive and Well But Barely Able to
    Walk   66
Thinking of Frost   134
Thinning the Spruces   185
Thomas, Barbara   53
To the Old Maples   47
Tobin, Daniel   80
Torres, Angela Narciso   93
Transmission   189
Tree Ghost   67
Tree *(Hirshfield)*   68
Tree *(Seshadri)*   74
Trespass   168
Trethewey, Natasha   94
Turner, Brian   165
Tuszynska, Emily   122
Under the Linden   176
Vertical   150
Veil   111
Wanek, Connie   86, 114
Warren, Rosanna   193
Watching Blackbirds Turn to Ghosts   128
Weaver, Afaa Michael   136
What is Left   62
What Isn't There   93
What I've Learned about Cottonwoods   163
where you are planted   19
White Petals, 3 A.M.   100

Whited, Gary   30
Williams, Leslie   124
Wilson, Joyce   192
Winter   142
Young, C. Dale   125
Zamora, Javier   58
Zetzel, Geraldine   96
Zisquit, Linda Stern   181

CPSIA information can be obtained
at www.ICGtesting.com
Printed in the USA
BVHW040930280622
640810BV00007B/150